SELF-DEFENSE & ASSAULT F
for GIRLS & WOMEN is a complete course of basic
self-defense especially developed to meet the
needs and capabilities of girls and women living
in the modern world.

This is self-defense viewed as a safety and health
concern, with emphasis on assault prevention.
This is self-defense presented as an aspect of
competence and self-reliance. A major objective
of this text is to teach attitudes, behavior and
procedures to minimize the possibility of becoming a victim. The physical defenses are simple
techniques which anyone can learn.

Physical education instructors and professionals
in the field of counseling and guidance have
praised the authors for their sound advice,
practical techniques, rational goals, and for their
ethical concepts.

This book is a completely new version of an
earlier work by the same authors. In this version,
there is greater emphasis on assertive responses
for assault deterrence, and new material on
prevention of sexual assault.

"...should be required reading for all girls and women..."
              WILSON LIBRARY BULLETIN

*"...simple and straightforward with no condescension...
easy to learn and viable as defense tactics..."*
              SCHOOL LIBRARY JOURNAL

*"Learning self-defense is primarily the process of learning
how to avoid becoming a victim...is the philosophy behind
this excellent manual..."*
              KLIATT PAPERBACK BOOK GUIDE

BOOKS BY BRUCE TEGNER

BRUCE TEGNER'S COMPLETE BOOK of SELF-DEFENSE

BRUCE TEGNER'S COMPLETE BOOK of KARATE

BRUCE TEGNER'S COMPLETE BOOK of JUDO

BRUCE TEGNER'S COMPLETE BOOK of AIKIDO

BRUCE TEGNER'S COMPLETE BOOK of JUKADO

BRUCE TEGNER'S COMPLETE BOOK of JUJITSU

SELF-DEFENSE: A BASIC COURSE

SELF-DEFENSE for YOUR CHILD (With Alice McGrath)
Elementary school age boys & girls

SELF-DEFENSE and ASSAULT PREVENTION for
GIRLS & WOMEN (With Alice McGrath)

SELF-DEFENSE NERVE CENTERS & PRESSURE POINTS

KARATE: Self-Defense & Traditional Sport Forms

KARATE & JUDO EXERCISES

STICK-FIGHTING: SPORT FORMS

STICK-FIGHTING: SELF-DEFENSE

BLACK BELT JUDO, KARATE, JUKADO

AIKIDO and Jiu Jitsu Holds & Locks

SAVATE: French Foot & Fist Fighting

JUDO: Sport Techniques for Physical Fitness & Tournament

DEFENSE TACTICS for LAW ENFORCEMENT:
Weaponless Defense & Control and Baton Techniques

KUNG FU & TAI CHI: Chinese Karate & Classical Exercise

Additional titles in preparation

SELF-DEFENSE &
ASSAULT PREVENTION
for GIRLS & WOMEN

BRUCE TEGNER & ALICE McGRATH

THOR PUBLISHING COMPANY
P. O. BOX 1782
VENTURA, CALIFORNIA 93001

Library of Congress Cataloging in Publication Data

Tegner, Bruce.
  Self-defense & assault prevention for girls & women.

  1. Self-defense for women. [1. Self-defense for
women] I. McGrath, Alice Greenfield, 1917-   joint
author. II. Title.
GV1111.5.T44   796.8'1   76-39853
ISBN 0-87407-515-7
ISBN 0-87407-026-0 pbk.

First edition: February 1977
Second printing: April 1977
Third printing: January 1978
Fourth printing: January 1980

SELF-DEFENSE & ASSAULT PREVENTION
for GIRLS & WOMEN

by BRUCE TEGNER & ALICE McGRATH

THOR PUBLISHING COMPANY
   POST OFFICE BOX 1782
VENTURA, CALIFORNIA 93001

Printed in the
United States
of America

BRUCE TEGNER BOOKS REVIEWED

SELF-DEFENSE: A BASIC COURSE
"An eminently practical, concise guide to self-defense intended
for young men not versed in the martial arts . . ."
American Library Association BOOKLIST

BRUCE TEGNER'S COMPLETE BOOK OF SELF-DEFENSE
Recommended for Y.A. in the American Library Association
BOOKLIST

BRUCE TEGNER'S COMPLETE BOOK OF JUDO
"...the definitive text...ideal for instructors and individuals."
SCHOLASTIC COACH

BRUCE TEGNER'S COMPLETE BOOK OF JUJITSU
"...authoritative and easy-to-follow text...clear photos."
SCHOOL LIBRARY JOURNAL

KARATE: Self-defense & Traditional Forms
Recommended for Y.A. in the American Library Association
BOOKLIST

BRUCE TEGNER'S COMPLETE BOOK OF KARATE
"Tegner suggests and illustrates changes to bring karate in
line with modern concepts of physical education...invaluable
for teaching karate in schools, colleges and recreation centers."
CAPHER

SELF-DEFENSE FOR YOUR CHILD (with Alice McGrath)
[For elementary school age boys & girls]
"...informative, readable book for family use..."
CHRISTIAN HOME & SCHOOL

"...intelligent, clear-headed approach..." BOOKS WEST

SELF-DEFENSE & ASSAULT PREVENTION FOR GIRLS & WOMEN (with
Alice McGrath)
"...should be required reading for all girls and women..."
WILSON LIBRARY BULLETIN
"...simple and straightforward with no condescension...easy to
learn and viable as defense tactics..." SCHOOL LIBRARY JOURNAL

BRUCE TEGNER'S COMPLETE BOOK OF JUKADO
"This is the most useful book on the Oriental fighting arts I
have ever seen." LIBRARY JOURNAL

SELF-DEFENSE NERVE CENTERS & PRESSURE POINTS
"Students and teachers will find much valuable source
material in this attractive book." SCHOLASTIC COACH

DEFENSE TACTICS FOR LAW ENFORCEMENT
". . . a practical tool for police academy programs, police
science programs at the university level, and for the (individual)
officer . . ." THE POLICE CHIEF

KUNG FU & TAI CHI: Chinese Karate and Classical Exercise
"...recommended for physical fitness collections."
LIBRARY JOURNAL

ACKNOWLEDGMENTS

The authors wish to thank:

JAN GOLDBERG
JEFF HAGER
MARY ANNE HESSEL
DRENDA JOHNSON
KELLY McENROE
MAUREEN MAHONEY
HELEN PHILLIPS
DON PHILLIPS
HERK ROSSILLI
DANIEL SCHNEIDER
REGINALD SHEPHARD
CAROL WEINSTOCK

for demonstrating the defenses in this book.

We would like to express our appreciation to the Women's Physical Education Workshop, *at California Polytechnic College, San Luis Obispo, California, where our original physical education course was introduced in 1967.*

BEVERLY BOWMAN and BARBARA BOYD *were the first to validate our theories in the classroom. We extend special thanks to them for their confidence and support.*

CONTENTS

We educate one another; and we cannot do this if half of us consider the other half not good enough to talk to.

GEORGE BERNARD SHAW

INTRODUCTION

Self-defense does not begin with the act of striking back; it starts with concepts of self-respect, self-reliance and autonomy. Self-respect is the feeling that your individual self is worth defending from assault; self-reliance is the conviction that you are competent to take care of yourself; autonomy implies that you are able to make decisions for yourself and take responsibility for your health and well-being.

The question "Does a woman lose her femininity if she learns self-defense?" implies that femininity is synonymous with passivity, docility, helplessness and dependence.

The helpless woman, more alluringly feminine as she is more helpless, is a stereotype woman. The statement that women (all women) are helpless is in conflict with reality. Neither men nor women can be defined as inherently passive or dominant; neither men nor women are inherently self-reliant or dependent. Every culture has its definition of what constitutes feminine behavior. What the culture expects is what it gets - on the surface. The expectations and definitions for male and female behavior are different in different parts of the world and in different times; the differences in expectations have produced a wide range of behavior. When any group is generally viewed as helpless creatures who cannot protect themselves, the prediction of helplessness comes true; it is a self-fulfilling prophecy. It comes true for women not because of inherent incompetence; it comes true when girls are assigned a role, trained in that role, and grow up to become women who believe in that role.

There would be no competent women if helplessness and dependence were inborn traits; there would be no passive, dependent men if aggressiveness and dominance were inborn traits.

Women are increasingly facing the reality that they have
the capacity to take care of themselves and that they need
to develop their capacities into learned competence. They
are increasingly realizing that they need to take responsibility for themselves if they are to fulfill their potentials
as human beings.

They are becoming increasingly aware that self-respect,
self-reliance and autonomy are the basis for good
relationships -- including good relationships with men.

IS SELF-DEFENSE INSTINCTIVE?

Most of what we know is learned. We learn from instruction or through observation and much of what we call
"instinctive" behavior is behavior we learn at such an
early age that we do not recall the process of learning it.

You do not know how to swim instinctively. You do
not know how to escape from a burning building by
instinct. Instinct does not tell you how to give simple
first-aid. You are taught basic swimming to protect you
from drowning; you take fire drill to cope with the emergency of fire; you learn first-aid through instruction.

The techniques and procedures and physical actions
which minimize danger of assault and which are effective against assault are not instinctive in either men or
women. If the ability to defend oneself were a natural
"manly" attribute, then all men could defend themselves.
Self-defense is neither masculine nor feminine; it is a
learned skill and anyone can learn it. It is not particularly
complicated or difficult, but it is not automatic. It
must be learned!

SELF-DEFENSE: A Definition

Almost anyone can learn practical self-defense in a fairly short time without becoming an expert fighter. This point of view is based on many years of experience in the field.

The principal obstacles to teaching and learning self-defense are concepts and practices which are out-dated and inappropriate, but which are still widely accepted.

One way of defining practical self-defense is to clarify what it is *not*. Self-defense is not warfare; it is not personal vengeance; it is not a way of life; it is not a TV or movie fight scene.

Self-defense instruction is preparation to minimize the possibility of assault; it is training to learn and use a small group of simple, effective physical actions if no other alternative is available. Learning self-defense is primarily the process of learning how to avoid becoming a victim.

The view that self-defense instruction is preparation to become a skilled fighter has the effect of eliminating those who most need to learn how to protect themselves. All of the traditional forms of fighting set a high level of skill as their goal and that is one of the reasons that traditional fighting methods (boxing, karate, aikido, kung fu and others) are not suitable for basic self-defense.

Our capabilities must bear some relationship to real life goals. Women learning to defend themselves ought not to be treated as though they were going to war. The legal and moral definition of self-defense expressly limits the degree of force to the *least* amount which can be used to avert or stop an assault. Warfare training is preparation to use the *maximum* amount of force.

Punitive responses to violence do not contribute solutions; they escalate violence. Personal vengeance is not consistent with law-abiding citizenship. It is understandable that some individuals take violent action when they are severely frustrated, but personal vengeance destroys the law. It is dangerous to live in a community which ignores laws in favor of vigilante action. Vengeance is self-defeating; the consequences of acts of personal revenge are always tragic.

DENIAL, OBSESSION or COMPETENCE

Because practical self-defense has not been made widely available to women and because self-defense has been confused with sport judo, karate fighting, aikido, police defense tactics and other inappropriate combat skills, many women have taken refuge in denial, or they have become tormented by obsession.

Denial is a refusal to think about or prepare for the emergency of threatened assault because the thought is too frightening. Denial may take the form of reckless disregard for prudent behavior, or it may be expressed by the pretense that no danger exists.

Obsession is never-ending concern with the danger of assault. The individual who is obsessed with anxiety about assault lives under the flag of catastrophe - always expecting the worst; life is distorted through a fog of suspicion. An enormous amount of energy is wasted; obsession is self-defeating.

Reckless denial and obsessive anxiety prevent realistic assessments of the danger of assault and they interfere with positive preparation to minimize the possibility and cope with the actuality of assault.

A major objective of this course is education for health and safety, to relieve anxiety and reduce fear. Competence is developed through learning appropriate responses to aggression, ranging from verbal assertiveness to defense actions against serious assault. When women learn how to minimize the possibility of assault, they develop a sense of proportion.

With preparation to cope with the emergency of threatened assault, there is no need to deny the danger. When careful, preventive procedures are known, obsessive anxiety can be reduced to prudent concern.

TELEVISION & SELF-IMAGE

On television and in the movies, girls and women are consistently portrayed as victims. Even when the point of view is essentially sympathetic, television fiction, news stories and even documentaries focus on the most extreme cases of brutal assault. The victim is always shown as helpless to prevent the assault and powerless to resist.

Seeing themselves repeatedly depicted as passive victims, and regularly viewing (and reading about) the most terrifying assaults, has a devastating effect on girls and women. They are exposed to daily reinforcement of feelings of powerlessness and a growing sense of anxiety and dread. Those who watch many hours of television tend to exaggerate the danger of assault in real life; they tend to be confused about the sources of danger; they tend to underestimate their ability to cope with danger.

In real life, women are not the most helpless victims of assault. If any segment of the population can be characterized as vulnerable, it is children. Children are subject to assault from their peers and from any adult, including their parents. [1]

The aged, the infirm, the disabled are frequently lumped into the category "vulnerable," but if you look to real life for examples, you will find considerable evidence among them of self-reliance and a refusal to be victimized.

In fact, the most numerous victims of assault are young men -- and this is not reflected in the mass media, nor is it publicized in articles about violence.

To characterize all females - half the population! - as vulnerable is clearly untrue and irrational. Television portrays women as vulnerable not because it is accurate, but because it makes for gory, dramatic, exciting stories which shock and horrify - and raise the ratings. While

[1] The subject of parental (or other adult) assault on children does not come within the scope of self-defense, but peer or bully assault is covered in our book: SELF-DEFENSE for YOUR CHILD [for elementary school age boys and girls] (Ventura, Calif., Thor Pub. Co., 1976).

raising the ratings, it lowers the morale of the women
viewers, making them fearful, anxious and hopeless.

In real life, assaults range from annoying or humiliating,
to moderately serious, to extremely dangerous and vicious.
Because the assaults most frequently seen on the screen
are very serious, and often fatal, it is implied that deadly
assaults are commonplace.

On the screen, victims rarely demonstrate successful
resistance, leaving viewers with the impression that
resistance is impractical, ineffective, or impossible.
In fact, resistance is successful in a high proportion
of attempted assaults.

Young girls who watch television for many hours a day
are more susceptible than boys to feelings of terror and
powerlessness. Watching television, girls infer that they
have little or no control over their lives - that they are
at the mercy of men, who are cast in the confusing,
ambiguous role of protector/assailant.

Boys can, and some do, identify with the actor who performs
the role of the dominant adult male (which is not without its
special hazards!).

Girls who see themselves portrayed as perpetual prey at any
age, must overcome a serious impediment to their growth and
development in order to achieve that most significant
characteristic of adulthood - self-reliance.

DON'T BE A WILLING VICTIM

There are two actors in the assault drama - the aggressor and
the victim. The aggressor assigns the roles. He casts himself
as the domineering male and he assigns the role of helpless
victim to his intended prey. Although the aggressor assigns
the parts, you may accept or reject his choice of you as his

victim. If you accept the part, you become a *willing* victim and you ensure the success of his plan. If you reject the role, that decision *alone* may be the decisive factor in your successful defense.

You can choose another role. You can choose to cope with the situation. Whether the solution is escape, verbal assertion or physical defense will be determined by the circumstances. No matter what action you take, it is the fact that you have made a choice not to be a willing victim which is essential for your safety.

We have become too accustomed to the notion that if someone says, or seems to threaten, "I am going to hit you," we must choose between submissive behavior (cowering down, crying, pleading) or aggressive behavior (counter-threats). The most effective response is: "No! You are *not* going to hit me." The refusal to be drawn into the game of abuser-or-abused is a positive, rational and ethical response.

Assaults differ in kind, degree of force used, resulting injury and in purpose. Assailants differ in many ways. Victims also differ in fundamental characteristics, but a large proportion of victims have one thing in common: They are docile. Many victims have allowed themselves to be victimized because they have not been educated or prepared to cope with the emergency of threatened assault; they do not understand that immediate, firm, determined refusal to be intimidated is their most potent protection against assault.

There are a few exceptions to this general rule (see: When to Defend Against an Armed Assailant) but there is considerable evidence to support the view that spirited resistance is safer than submissive compliance.

Never plead with an assailant; it simply assures him of your helplessness. Even though you might be frightened - and it is frightening to be threatened with assault - you can show determination to protect yourself once you realize that assertive behavior is more effective than hopeless submission.

WOMEN AS LOSERS/WOMEN AS WINNERS

Because women are so often portrayed as losers, a reaction against this demeaning view is to encourage women to think of themselves as winners. In competitive sports this is a corrective and appropriate measure; in the area of self-defense, it is counter-productive. To compare an assault with a sport or contest is to mis-state the relationship between the assailant and the intended victim. Assault is not a sporting event; self-defense should not be classified with or confused with sport or contest.

Participants in a sport contest have agreed to compete; they have trained for the event; they are bound by a set of known rules which apply to both contestants equally.

Contestants train in the expectation of meeting an opponent of approximately equal skill. In most sporting events there are safeguards against injury and in most sports, any deliberate effort to cause injury is a foul. The objectives in a sport are to compete (observing the rules, demonstrating the highest level of skill) and to win!

There are no referees, spectators or rules of sportsmanship in an assault. With preparation to cope with the threat of assault, there is less likelihood that physical actions will be used at all! In a sport fight the assumption is that the competition will take place; our self-defense instruction is based on the assumption that escape or avoidance would be the first choice response.

"Winning" is an irrelevant concept for practical self-defense. If women had to "win" a fight with men as a condition for learning self-defense, only the exceptional woman could learn to defend herself. The view that self-defense instruction is preparation to become a skilled fighter has the effect of barring those individuals who have the greatest need. Those individuals who are unable or unwilling to become expert fighters benefit from the study of practical self-defense to the greatest degree.

Successful resistance to assault does not mean winning a fight with a man; it means demonstrating determination to avoid the role of docile, passive victim!

IS A LITTLE INSTRUCTION A DANGEROUS THING?

We still hear arguments against teaching basic self-defense on the curious grounds that it is better to know nothing at all than it is to have functional skill. Those who hold this strange view cannot imagine self-defense as anything except preparation to win a contest-like fight with a larger, stronger opponent. Men will state their opposition to self-defense by saying, "I don't want my daughter or wife to learn the manly art of self-defense. They can stay away from hazardous places, or they can run away or bite, and scratch."

The men who see themselves as needing to "cherish and protect" their daughters and wives, and the daughters and wives who accept that banality, are living in a world of rhetoric and fantasy. In the real world, fathers and husbands of assault victims have been nowhere near their beloved, helpless females when they were being assaulted. The only way that a man can "protect" a woman is to be at her side every moment, making a prisoner of the woman and a full-time guard of the man.

Staying away from dangerous places is a prudent thing to do and we strongly advise it, when it is possible. It is not practical advice for millions of girls and women who have to go to school and work in areas (no longer so easy to define and avoid) where there is a possibility of street assault. Even in high crime areas, the *majority* of the residents are concerned with the problem as potential victims, not as offenders.

Scratching and biting are not the most effective defenses, though they are better than passive non-resistance.

Another curious assumption made by those who oppose basic self-defense is that women who have basic skills will over-estimate their abilities, will take greater risks than they are prepared to handle, and that they will suffer from over-confidence.

Girls and women who are instructed in appropriate, modern, functional self-defense do not become combative; they become more prudent. To propose that a woman who is

cornered, unable to run or get help, should be totally
ignorant about how to defend herself - and that is preferable
to knowing basic techniques - simply does not make sense.

Women do not become victims because of "over-confidence,"
they become victims because of panic helplessness.

Panic helplessness is a major cause of drownings, death in
fires, earthquakes and other disasters. Unless people are
drilled in life-saving procedures they do not always do the
right thing if they are confronted with danger.

Those who are prepared to cope with emergency situations
are less likely to panic. Those who have no preparation to
cope with frightening emergency are the most susceptible to
panic helplessness. Even in situations which are relatively
simple to manage and in which the danger of physical harm
is not great, panic blocks positive actions. Panic induces a
sense of powerlessness which may be out of proportion to
the threatened danger.

Self-defense instruction does not increase recklessness; it
diminishes the possibility of panic.

WHY NOT RUN AWAY?

Running away is a prudent and sensible way to avoid
assault - if you can do it! Running away from an assailant
is an option to be chosen whenever possible. Learning
physical defense actions does not mean that you are
committed to stay and resist if you have a way to escape;
any prudent person would choose escape!

If you are cornered, you cannot run. If there is no safe
place to run to, it is imprudent to run. If there is no safe
place to run to, the assailant will interpret running as
victim behavior. Turning your back on an assailant is
practical only if you judge that you can outrun him and
that you can reach a safe destination. Otherwise it is
more prudent to show assertive self-control, and be
prepared to use defense techniques, if necessary.

SELF-DEFENSE and FRIENDS & RELATIVES

Is self-defense effective against friends and relatives? The question is actually three separate questions with three different answers.

A. Is it possible to demonstrate (prove) self-defense techniques with friends?

B. Is it possible to use self-defense when the aggressor is a friend?

C. Is it possible to use self-defense against repeated assaults by a husband, relative or friend?

To answer these questions in order:

A. Resist the temptation to show off your new skill. The techniques are effective when they are applied with earnest intent and with the appropriate vigor and spirit. A defense which requires a kick into the shin, for instance, will not produce the necessary effect without the kick. If you kick your friend vigorously, it hurts; if you do not kick, the defense fails. Another reason for not trying out defenses with friends is that you give an advantage to your mock opponent by inviting the assault (challenging) - something you would never do in actual defense. Unexpectedness is a significant factor in assault-resistance; when you try to show off a defense technique, you lose the element of surprise.

B. Knowing a range of responses from verbal command to vigorous physical defense actions lets you choose a solution which is appropriate to the situation. When you have a choice of responses, you do not have to treat every case of aggression as though it were a vicious attack. If a friend becomes angry and threatens assault, you can respond with an appropriate defense. But defenses against friends must be particularly earnest and unambiguous. If you make gestures of defense at the same time that you give signals of compliance (smiling or giggling), you are not resisting effectively.

C. If someone with whom you have a very close relationship (husband, relative, steady boyfriend) attempts assault, you could defend yourself with any of the verbal or physical techniques in this course. But if the possibility of assault is a permanent feature of the relationship, you need a different kind of help. Young girls who maintain ongoing relationships with men who assault them become wives whose husbands beat them. Change of some kind is necessary to solve the problem. Some of the options are: Negotiation, counseling, therapy or separation. Question C ought to be restated as: What kind of changes can be made to *eliminate* assault as a feature of the relationship?

DOES TEACHER NEED A BLACK BELT?

Because many of the actions of self-defense derive from Asian forms of weaponless fighting, there is (a mistaken) belief that the people who teach it ought to be experts in karate, judo, aikido or a related skill, in order to qualify as instructors. The black belt, which symbolizes high proficiency in the martial arts, is regarded by some as a prerequisite for teaching *any* form of self-defense.

The black belt requirement for teaching is an outmoded tradition which is not pertinent to modern, basic self-defense. Black belt ratings indicate excellence in performance. A black belt does not represent teaching ability. Belt ratings are awarded for winning in contest or for demonstration of technical achievement. The ability to compete or perform is not the same as the ability to teach.

A physical education teacher is better prepared to teach basic self-defense than is a black belt holder who has not had formal teacher training and whose ideas and methods might not be consistent with modern concepts of health and physical education. There is a good deal more to teaching than the performance of skills which the students are required to imitate. Particularly in the teaching of self-defense for women, patience, empathy and the ability to communicate and to encourage are more important than performance proficiency. A black belt is not awarded for those qualities which make fine teachers.

Men and women physical education instructors are qualified to teach basic self-defense whether or not they have special training in a martial art. The traditional martial arts do not prepare teachers to teach the fundamentals of practical self-defense. Physical education teachers are not required to be champion swimmers in order to teach and coach swimming; they are not required to be outstanding performers of track events in order to teach them. They can and do teach highly successful self-defense classes by virtue of their skill and experience in *teaching*.

Where the black belt is considered a qualification for teaching self-defense, the most appropriate teachers are disqualified. Few physical education teachers have black belt ratings. Of those who do, even fewer are women. Women physical education teachers in California were pioneers in teaching basic self-defense to girls and women. They understood the need and had the courage to experiment. They were the first to validate our theory that physical education classes provide the best and most suitable environment for self-defense training. Physical education teachers have the greatest opportunity and the most favorable setting for teaching self-defense as an aspect of health and personal development and they don't need a black belt to do it.

PARTNERS

To practice the defense actions it is best to have a cooperating partner. It is not necessary to have a real emergency in order to teach correct responses to emergency situations. People learn cardio-vascular and mouth-to-mouth rescusitation using artificial models in practice; we do not drown our partners in order to practice life-saving. It is not necessary to practice defense actions against a real assailant.

In contest training, where the objective is to fight a competing adversary, it is appropriate to *compete* with a partner in order to develop competition skill. Self-defense can be learned with a passive or cooperating partner; a non-cooperative partner makes learning difficult.

Women partners, men partners, or men and women working together can learn self-defense if there is mutual concern and helpfulness. If men partners condescend to women partners, or try to prevent successful simulation of the defense, or exhibit discomfort in acting out the role of assailant, the atmosphere and environment will not be conducive to learning.

Partners can be assigned according to the situation (available partners), according to the students' preference (are they more at ease with a partner of their own sex) and the teacher's preference and experience.

We have found that women partners work very well together. This is particularly so in those instances where women are struggling to overcome feelings of inadequency.

Although we have elected to illustrate most of the defenses using men to demonstrate the assault, our most successful classes for women have been those in which women work with women partners. In co-educational classes this can be done by matching men with male partners and women with female partners. As the class progresses, students and teacher can determine which of the men can work with women as cooperative, helpful partners and which men and women are unable to work together comfortably. Some women make better progress if they work exclusively with women partners and others do very well if they have an opportunity to practice with men.

It is not necessary to wear any special uniforms for the practice of self-defense, nor is it necessary to work on a mat. Any ordinary firm floor will do. Our classes usually practice barefoot as an extra safety precaution; if accidental contact is made during kicking practice, there is less possibility of partners hurting each other.

THE BASIC DEFENSE ACTIONS

Instead of learning a specific defense for every specific assault, you will learn a handful of defense actions which can be combined in a flexible way, and used in a manner which is appropriate to the situation. You will be prepared to cope with a variety of common assaults without having to learn hundreds of attack-and-defense tricks.

The few exceptions to the flexible-response method will be pointed out in the text; they are for serious situations in which the given defense is the most effective and the easiest to learn. For the most part, after you have learned the relatively simple basic defense actions, you will practice examples of different combinations of these actions and then you will be able to improvise your own combinations for use against a wide range of assaults.

The advantage of learning to respond in a flexible way is that you do not have to stop to think "What is the right defense in this situation?" You can act immediately, using any of the actions which are appropriate and possible. You will then have available to you, literally, thousands of defenses, without having to memorize rigid sequences of actions in specific order.

Look at the photos showing the twelve fundamental defense actions and you will see that they are quite simple. There are no complicated holds and locks, no spectacular throws, no power punches, no ceremonial procedures. You will see that all of the basic defense actions can be used by a smaller person against a larger aggressor. The defense actions do not rely on superior strength or power for their effectiveness. You are not learning an art; you are learning a practical skill!

Here is a summary of the physical defense actions
which you will learn:

1. How to hit with the side of your fist.
2. How to use the heel of your palm.
3. How to hit with the edge of your open hand
    (the chop).
4. How to hit (or parry) with your forearm.
5. How to escape wrist grips.
6. How to use finger-bending for release of grips
    or chokes.
7. How to use an elbow blow.
8. How to use a slapping parry.
9. How to use stabbing finger blows.
10. How to kick with the edge of your shoe.
11. How to stamp-kick downward.
12. How to stamp-kick with the bottom of your shoe.

1. How to hit with   2. How to use the heel
the side of your fist.   of your palm.

3. How to hit with the edge of your open hand (the chop).

4. How to hit (or parry) with your forearm.

5. How to escape wrist grips.

6. How to use finger-bending for release of grips or chokes.

7. How to use an elbow
blow.

8. How to use a slapping
parry.

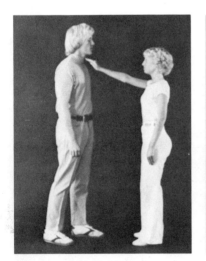

9. How to use stabbing
finger blows.

10. How to kick with the
edge of your shoe.

| 11. How to stamp-kick downward. | 12. How to stamp-kick with the bottom of your shoe. |

SAFETY IN PRACTICE

There is no need for either partner to be hurt in the practice of self-defense.

Many of the techniques are very painful if they are applied realistically and some are impossible to practice as they would be used in actual defense against assault. This is simulation training. Simulation practice is a successful method in a variety of emergency preparation courses.

The practice sessions are not intended to *prove* the techniques; they are intended to help you rehearse and learn them.

Although the photos show contact blows to illustrate how the defense would be used, you and your partner will either touch very lightly, to simulate the blow, or you will not make contact at all, depending on the technique and on the specific instruction for safe practice.

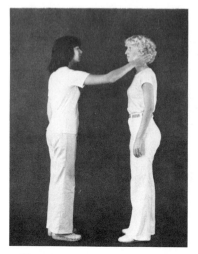

13

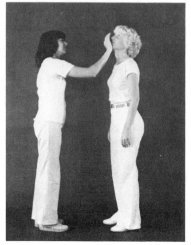

14

15

When you are learning how and where to hit, you may
touch your partner very lightly and gently; this is a
first step in learning the action, the target area and
the body movement. You will be taking turns with
your partner; you help each other by standing passively
in the first stage of practice.

13, 14, 15. The partner practicing the actions works in slow
motion to rehearse the gesture of one and then another hand
blow and an elbow blow.

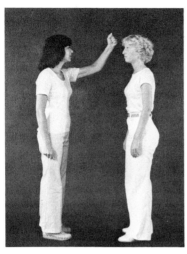 

16   17

16. You can practice the *gesture* of a vigorous blow without making contact. It is the forcefulness of your action, your body gesture and your expression which are realistic.

17. A special caution: Follow the rules of safety when practicing any of the defense actions, but you must be particularly careful to stay away from the throat and eyes in simulation of defenses against serious assault. A light finger contact-blow to the eye is dangerous. A forceful hand blow to the throat or eye is a very high-risk-of-injury tactic. It is reserved for defense against a highly serious assault. Do not come any closer than shown in this photo when simulating such techniques.

Further along in the text, you will be given instructions for practicing full-power hand and foot blows using improvised training equipment, if you wish to do so.

For safe practice, when you are first learning the kicking techniques, you may touch your partner very lightly, just to establish the correct foot position and the target. When you practice lively kicking techniques, do not come close to kicking your partner. Even a moderate kick into the shin is painful; a forceful kick is extremely painful.

18

19

18, 19. You can learn gesture without contact, as in the photos.

A highly trained individual can deliver fast, powerful and accurate blows to within a fraction of an inch of a target point, without making contact. For practical self-defense training, that kind of skill is neither necessary nor appropriate.

Some of the parrying and wrist-grip releases will be done with contact and with a degree of realism, but when you are instructed to hit or kick, *simulate* a hit or kick.

Don't Rush

A good way of learning self-defense techniques is to work slowly. In beginning practice, especially, you will learn better and ensure safe practice if you work at a pace compatible with your skill. For many people, working slowly is a much better way of assimilating the material. A technique which is learned in proper form can be speeded up with relatively little practice; if you rush through, you may fail to learn the action in its most effective application.

HOW & WHERE TO HIT

Before beginning to practice the techniques with your partner, be sure that you understand the safety procedures. You are not preparing to win a fight; you are rehearsing responses to possible aggression to show that you will not accept the role of passive victim.

The photos show contact: When you make contact on your partner, it is with a very light touch, just to learn where to hit and to practice the correct action. When you simulate the action with a vigorous gesture, do *not* come close to hitting your partner.

Side of Fist

20. Using the side of your fist, hit down onto the bridge of the nose. This is a limited-use blow - the only practical target is down onto the nose, and you should use it only if you are already close in - but it is easily used and it is effective, even if the assailant is considerably taller and stronger than you.

Moderate force can be used, or, if appropriate, it can be delivered as a full-power, smashing blow.

20

Open-Hand Blow - The Chop, or Slash

The open-hand blow, familiarly known as the chop or
slash, is a practical, versatile basic technique with
many advantages for functional self-defense: You
can use it up close, or out of the hitting range of an
assailant. You can modify the force of the blow to
suit the circumstances, using a moderately forceful
blow when that would be appropriate, and a forceful blow, if necessary.

You can learn to hit a full-force blow without hurting
your own hand. You can use either hand for delivering
an effective chop.

A significant advantage is that you can be ready to
use this hand blow without assuming a posture of
belligerence or challenge, thus giving you the opportunity of taking control through verbal assertiveness
without losing the protection of being ready to make
a physical defense, if necessary.

Because of individual hand structure, the correct hitting
position will be slightly different for each person. The
basic position is: Your hand is held firm, but not rigid;
it is slightly cupped; fingers and thumb are pressed
together - do not extend the thumb. The striking area
is the fleshy, padded portion of the edge of your hand,
half-way between your wrist bone and your little finger;
your hand is at a slight angle to the target area.

To find the position which is correct for your hand,
experiment in the following manner: First, remove
rings, bracelets, watches and other ornaments, for
safety. Holding your hand in the general position
described above, hit very lightly onto a hard surface
such as a table top or a floor.

When hitting with slight force, you should feel no contact
onto your wrist bone or onto your little finger bones;
only the fleshy part of your hand (slightly to the inside
of your palm) should be making contact. Shift the angle
of your hand, tipping it forward to avoid hitting your
wrist bone, tipping it up to avoid hurting your little
finger. Adjust the angle until you feel only the protected,
padded part of your hand making contact.

21   22

When you feel that you are striking properly, gradually increase the force of your blow. If you feel a stinging sensation which lasts for only a few seconds, you are hitting correctly. If you feel pain which persists, you are making a mistake.

Work very slowly to develop the correct technique so that you will have confidence in your ability to use it with force. Hitting correctly, you will not hurt yourself if you deliver a full-force chop.

When you have learned the correct position for hitting with force, practice will develop speed. When you learn to hit as hard as you can as fast as you can - that is hard enough and fast enough for self-defense!

Where to Hit

The slashing open-hand blow can be delivered downward, cross-body, outward, upward, double-handed, with either hand.

The most practical targets for this hand blow are:

21. Down onto the bridge of the nose.

22. Up, under the nose, using a whipping action.

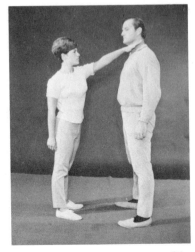

23   24

23. Into the side of the neck, hitting palm up...

24. ...or, with the same hand, hitting into the other side of the neck, delivering the blow palm down.

25. Double-handed, simultaneous blows can be effected into both sides of the neck.

26. Onto the mound of the forearm, using a downward cross-body blow, or into the bend of the elbow with the same action (not shown.)

27. Onto the wrist, downward, as shown, or back-handed.

28. Avoid this error.   If the thumb is extended, your hand position is awkward. You can deliver the most efficient open hand blow with the thumb and fingers together and your hand slightly cupped.

Partners take turns touching the target areas lightly, with the hand held in the correct position. Work slowly and carefully. Avoid hitting into the throat; even light blows are extremely painful and there is a high risk of injury if you strike the windpipe.[1]

[1]For a full description of the effects of blows at various body targets, see: SELF-DEFENSE NERVE CENTERS & PRESSURE POINTS, Tegner, B. (Ventura, CA, Thor Pub. Co., 1968).

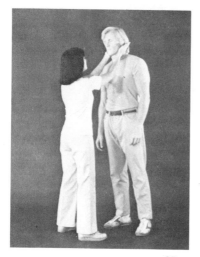

25

26

27

28

When you know the correct hand position for touching the target areas, practice the blows without making contact, but simulating vigorous, lively actions.

Practice to avoid reliance on your strong hand. If you are right-handed, practice left-handed blows to develop proficiency; if you are left-handed, do not neglect practice of right-handed slashing blows.

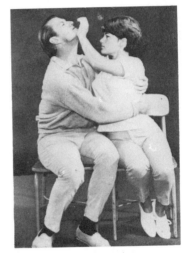

29   30

Heel-of-the-Palm Blow

29, 30. The heel of the palm can be used for a pushing action with moderate force, against an annoying person, or it can be delivered with a vigorous thrust up under the chin. Although it has limited application, it is effective, easy and practical. It can be used against a considerably taller assailant; it can be used seated or standing. An unexpected, lively heel-of-palm up under the chin could put an adversary off-balance, or on the ground.

In practice with your partner, simulate the pushing action; make contact, but observe the safety rules. Partner who takes the role of aggressor: Keep your mouth closed as an extra precaution. When practicing the lively, thrusting action, simulate the gesture but do not come close to your partner's chin.

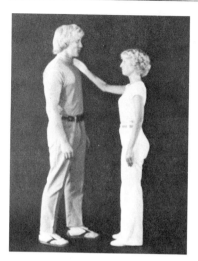 

31   32

Finger Stabs

Reserved for the most serious kinds of assaults, finger stabs into the throat or eyes are high-risk-of-injury actions. Even a slight blow into the eye may cause injury. A light blow or pressing action against the windpipe is extremely painful; a forceful blow could be fatal. Striking into the eyes or throat would be appropriate only in instances of extreme danger.

31. Touch the target area very lightly with the tips of your fingers.

32. Do *NOT* make contact; practice a slow-motion gesture of stabbing into the eye.

33. Just below the most exposed part of the windpipe, commonly called the Adam's apple, is a hollow in the throat which can be a target for a stabbing blow if the assault is vicious. Or, you can press very lightly with your fingertips.

For safety in practice, follow this procedure: The partner simulating the defense action places her fingertips at the throat hollow without applying pressure; the partner simulating the assailant moves forward slowly to experience the feeling of how little force is needed to result in pain. Pressing gently into this area is an effective way to move someone away from you.

34. Without coming close to your partner's throat, practice a vigorous, spirited finger stabbing gesture toward the throat.

35. Without coming close to your partner's eyes, make a stabbing gesture toward the target. Even when you do not come close to touching the eyes, an unexpected hand-thrust toward the eyes usually results in a reflex action of drawing the head back. This can be practiced with the fingers spread, as shown, or together as in photo 34.

Both partners must take responsibility for avoiding contact. The distance shown in photos 34 and 35 is as close as you should come (to the target area) when simulating lively actions directed at high risk body targets.

33

34

35

36   37

Elbow Blow

For practical self-defense, the elbow blow is used for
hitting at an assailant behind you.

36. Hitting with the tip of your elbow, strike very
lightly back into the midsection; make a fist and
turn it palm up, to deliver an efficient blow.

37. Looking around to see your target, with a
circular arm movement strike into the head or side
of the neck with the tip of your elbow. Make very
light contact.

To practice the elbow blow using vigorous gestures,
step forward away from your partner and simulate
the same blows without making contact.

38   39

Forearm Blow/Parry

38. The forearm can be used for hitting or for deflecting a reaching or grabbing arm. You can hit outward, as shown, or downward, or upward. The gesture is lively and vigorous; it is *not a pushing* action. Make a fist to deliver a more forceful blow.

39. A forearm parry blow can be used to stop an intended grab or reach from the back. Make a fist to deliver a more vigorous blow; let your body move naturally to follow the arm action.

Finger-Bending Grip Release

This release is effective against a strong grip. It can
be used with moderate force, when appropriate, and
it can be effected as a vigorous, lively action.

The efficiency of this technique is due to the fact
that you use the strength of your entire hand against
one finger of the gripping hand. If you pry one
finger loose, you can break the grip.

40. In practice, grip the little finger; it is the weakest.
In actual defense, if you could not grip the little
finger, this release will work against any one finger,
or against the thumb. But grip only one! Slowly
pull back on the finger until your partner releases.

Partners must cooperate to demonstrate the release
and do it without hurting each other. Partner acting
the role of assailant: Take a firm grip, but let go when
you feel that it is beginning to hurt. Do not maintain
your grip past the point when you realize that the
defense action is effective. Partner practicing the
defense: Work slowly; if you maintain a firm grasp
of the finger and maintain a slow, steady bending
pressure, you will be able to effect release.

41. This closeup shows the correct grip for the
finger-bending release.

42. Practice the same release against a finger choke,
as shown. Partner taking the turn of assailant: Take
a moderately firm grip, but do not dig your fingers
into your partner's throat. Defending partner: Grip
both little fingers with both your hands and use a
slow, steady action to effect release.

In defense against an assault, the release would be
effected with a snappy, vigorous action.

40

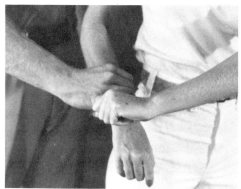

41

42

Slapping Parry

Because many hostile or aggressive actions start with
a reaching arm, this simple, deflecting parry is an
excellent response for stopping an intended assault.

The slapping parry has a wide range of applications; it
can be used to stop an annoying action and it can
deflect a fairly serious assault. It is easier to deflect
a grabbing or reaching arm than it is to block it. It is
simpler and more sensible to cope with the attempted
assault than to wait until the assault has been completed.
As the hostile action begins, respond with a whipping,
slapping parry, using the palm of your hand.

43. This is *not a pushing* action; it is a snappy, lively
slap. You can parry at the forearm...

44. ...or at the wrist. Practice using your left hand to
parry...

45. ...and parry with your right hand. In either case,
follow through to deflect the reaching arm completely
away from you.

The deflection, the determination shown in the facial
expression and the body gesture would be enough to
stop an assailant looking for a victim; this is self-reliant,
determined, non-victim response.

43

44

45

KICKING FOR SELF-DEFENSE

For use against serious assault attempts, a kick might be more practical, more effective and safer than hand blows.

If you are not already close in to the assailant, it is unwise to move in; kicking can be done without coming into the punching or grabbing range of a considerably larger individual.

46. Punching hand blows are not efficient when used by a smaller person against an assailant with a longer reach. If you had only hand blows to rely on, you would be limited to defense actions which would require moving in closer to the assailant.

47. There are situations in which it would be impossible to start a defense with hand blows; if, for instance, the assailant had gripped your wrists.

Kicking is effective because your leg is stronger than your arm; even a fairly slight person can deliver a kick with considerable force. Kicking is effective for practical self-defense, alone, or in conjunction with hand blows.

The kicks selected for self-defense are not the spectacular karate or kung fu kicking techniques which require strength, training and peak fitness.

The kicks for practical use are limited to those which most individuals can learn and use with functional efficiency. They can be remembered without constant practice. Peak physical fitness is not a requirement for practical use of self-defense kicks.

Kicking for self-defense gives you power, versatility, flexibility and efficiency.

48   49

How & Where to Kick

The two principal actions are: Snap-kicking with the edge of the shoe, and stamping with the bottom of the shoe.

First you will practice the gesture and learn the target areas in slow-motion simulation.

Edge-of-Shoe Kick

48. Using the edge of your shoe as the striking area, place your foot at your partner's shin (as though you had kicked into the shin) and with very light contact, scrape down the shin with the edge of your shoe...

49. ...and simulate a stamp onto the instep.

50. In slow motion, practice the same technique to the rear, placing the edge of shoe against your partner's shin...

51. ...and with a very light touch, scrape down the shin and simulate a stamp onto the instep.

50   51

52

Bottom-of-Shoe Kick

52. In slow motion, place the bottom of your shoe at your partner's knee, with your leg fully extended. Position yourself so that you can touch the knee target with the greatest possible distance between you and your partner.

53. Without taking a step, turn your upper body only, look around at your target area and simulate kicking into the knee of an assailant behind you. Practice carefully to avoid more than very light contact.

54. There are some instances when you would be able to use the bottom-of-the-shoe kick into the back of the knee. Place your foot at the back of your partner's knee and push lightly; you will feel how little force would be needed to put an assailant on the ground.

Snap-Kick Practice

The edge-of-the-shoe kick as used in self-defense is a
snappy, quick action. Because you are kicking into an
area highly vulnerable to pain, and using the shoe to
aid your action, a moderately forceful snap-kick is
remarkably effective.

After you have learned the correct foot position
and have touched the target area in slow motion
with your partner, proceed to practice the edge-of-
shoe kick in solo practice, or with your partner acting
as a reference point, but without making contact. A
class may practice this by making a circle and kicking
in toward an imaginary target point.

From a relaxed standing start, raise your foot about
six or eight inches off the floor; turn it so that the edge
of the outside of your shoe is the striking surface. Snap
the side of your foot toward the target, simulating a
sharp vigorous kick, aimed at the shin. Any part of the
shin, from just below the knee to just above the instep
is vulnerable; the prime target is the center of the shin-
bone, which is the most sensitive and exposed area.

Practice a snappy, quick action, putting your kicking
foot down immediately to avoid loss of balance. Alternate right and left foot practice to avoid reliance on
your strong side.

When you can perform one snap-kick with the edge of
your shoe with moderate proficiency, practice delivering
several kicks with the same foot without putting it on
the floor between kicks. In the section showing defenses
against example assaults, you will note that you could
easily deliver several forceful kicks without loss of
balance if you were gripped or held.

The first few times you practice the edge-of-shoe kick
into the shin of an imaginary assailant behind you, you
may find the action awkward. With a little practice,
you will realize how practical and useful it is to be able

to kick into the shin of an assailant gripping you from
behind. Your partner can help you by holding your
shoulder or your hand to help you maintain your balance when you first rehearse this action. Be careful:
Do not make contact on your partner's shin; it will be
very painful if you do.

When you are familiar with the action of the side-snap
kick to the rear, simulate a sharp, snappy kick into the
shin, following that action with a scrape down the shin
and then simulate a stamp onto the instep, with force,
but do not make contact onto your partner!

Stamping Kick

As a solo practice procedure, start from a relaxed standing
position, as though facing an assailant. Turn the side of
your body toward the target; raise your kicking leg with
the knee sharply bent and kick out with your leg fully
extended, hitting the (imaginary) knee with the bottom
of your shoe. This is a smashing action.

Put your kicking foot down onto the floor immediately,
to avoid losing your balance. Practice right and left foot
kicks. You need not kick any higher than the approxi-
mate knee height of an assailant - aim your kicks from
21 to 25 inches off the floor as a practice procedure. It
is less efficient to kick into the thigh than to kick into
the knee or shin; for practical defense, avoid kicking
higher than the knee.

When you can perform this kick with moderate proficiency, practice delivering two or more kicks with the
same foot before placing it onto the floor.

If you are practicing with a partner as your reference
point, be careful not to come too close to the target
area; kick with force and vigor, but stay far away from
your partner's knee. A class may practice this defense
action in a circle, kicking into the center at an imaginary target point.

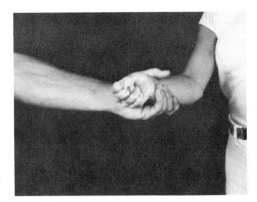

55

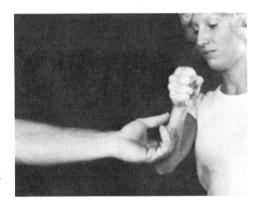

56

WRIST-GRIP RELEASES

Another technique for breaking wrist grips is an escape at the weakest area of the grip - from between the thumb and fore-finger of the gripping hand. If both wrists are gripped, you cannot use the finger-bending release; if one wrist is gripped, you can choose to use this escape or the finger-bending release.

55. With your partner, take turns demonstrating the difficulty of escaping by opposing force with force. Your partner grips your wrist as shown. Try to pull free by drawing your arm toward yourself; even a moderately strong grip can be maintained.

56. If, however, you snap your wrist away from between the thumb and forefinger, you can escape a moderately strong grip.

The success of the release depends on two factors: a sudden action and its direction. The manner in which the grip is taken will determine the direction of the escape; it should always be a snap from between the thumb and forefinger. The element of surprise helps the defense.

57. Both your wrists are gripped.

In beginning practice, your partner will take a firm grip but will allow you to escape if you perform the defense actions correctly.

The partner taking the role of assailant: Do not impede your partner's learning by refusing to release if the action is quick and snappy. Since you know in advance what the action will be, your partner cannot use the element of surprise.

58. Defending partner: Push outward, slightly, with both arms; in response to the outward push, the assailant will push inward. Going with the inward movement, move your wrists inward and then sharply up and out, bringing your hands toward your shoulders. Avoid pulling straight back; move your arms in an arc so that your wrists break free from between the thumbs and forefingers.

Against a very strong grip, you might have to precede the escape action with a forceful kick into the shin, to distract the assailant and help your defense. For the learning process, partners help each other by rehearsing the hand and arm actions accurately.

59. If one wrist is gripped, you may use the same principle with the help of your free hand. Make a fist of your captured hand and grip it with your free hand; snap out from between the thumb and the forefinger.

60. The strongest grip is a double-handed grip against one wrist. Make a fist of your captured hand; reach over and between the gripping arms to grip your own fist. With a jerky action, snap free in an upward or downward direction.

61. If the grip is taken so that the thumb and forefinger of the gripping hand are as shown, the direction of the release would be downward.

62. Gripping your captured hand with your free hand, snap down sharply.

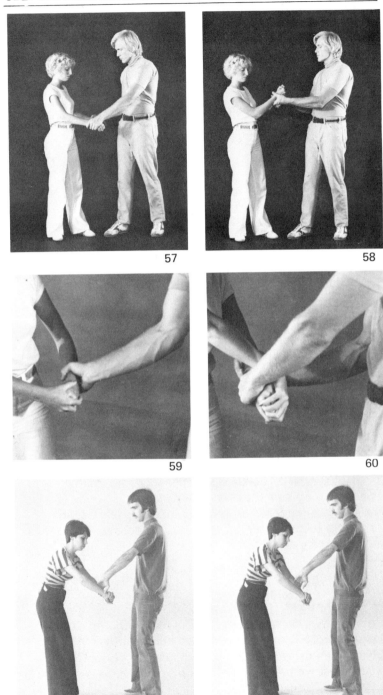

57

58

59

60

61

62

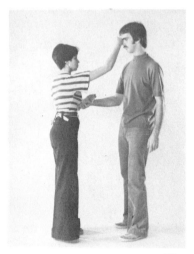 

63   64

THE ASSERTIVE *NO*

Most assaults made on girls and women are made by assailants
who are looking for easy targets; they do not want trouble,
they want passive victims. To make certain that they have
selected a passive person, assailants, in many cases, test the
intended victim with a spoken command, a threat, a threatening
gesture, or even a seemingly friendly overture. If the marked
victim responds with victim behavior, the assault is carried out;
non-victim behavior is a strong deterrent.

It is *imperative* not to delay an assertive response. Unless the
assailant is armed, docile obedience increases the danger of
assault. Stopping a threatened assault in the testing stage is
easier, more prudent, safer and more efficient. Orderly
resistance to an attempted assault is easier than escape from
a completed assault.

However, in order to respond with self-controlled assertiveness,
you have to be confident of your ability to use the defenses
in situations which are commonly thought of as "hopeless."
For example, there is a common perception of inevitable
helplessness if a woman is grabbed and held by a man.
Struggling - using strength against strength - is ineffective.
Since most women have not had preparation to cope with
this kind of situation, they are likely to display their feelings
of despair and allow themselves to be victimized.

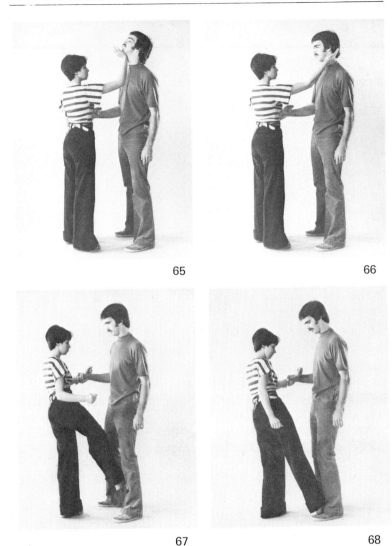

65   66

67   68

But there are, as you now know, a number of effective defense actions which can be taken. Among them:

63.64. Hitting onto the nose, or onto the gripping arm, or...

65,66. ...up under the chin, or slashing into the side of the neck, or...

67,68. ...kicking into the shin and scraping down.

69   70

69. A stamping kick into the knee is possible, and...

70. ...simultaneous hand and foot blows can be used.

The choice of techniques and the amount of force used would depend on the circumstances. But it is clear that *with preparation to cope,* helplessness is not inevitable.

71   72

71, 72. Even if you are lifted off the ground, you can use hand and foot blows.

Frequently, an assault begins with a command to "get in the car." Even when the assailant is unarmed, many women obey the command out of panic and because they have not been given instruction in how to deal with this sort of emergency. We rarely hear about the women who escape assault simply by refusing to go along, because that doesn't make a headline!

Because women often, automatically, defer to a man's polite, amiable overture, you should be aware of the danger of deferential behavior in risk environments. If a friendly stranger offers you a drink or asks for a light at a gathering in which you are comfortable and know the people, you are safe in assuming that you may offer the light or accept the refreshment. If a stranger in a dark parking lot asks you for a light, the prudent response is refusal and escape. If escape is not possible, your response should be refusal and readiness to demonstrate further verbal assertiveness and a readiness to resist.

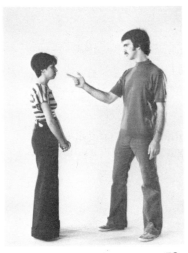 

73   74

73. The assailant makes a threatening gesture; the response is docile and passive, and affirms his choice of her as a victim.

74. The assailant makes a threat; her immediate response is active, positive and unambiguous: Stay away from me! Since he expects passivity and does not ordinarily know how to cope with assertiveness, this response might be all that would be necessary to cope effectively.

75   76

75, 76. The facial expression and the docile compliance shown here, plainly tell the assailant that he can expect passive, non-resisting behavior, ...

77, 78. ...while the opposite is shown in this response to the same situation; firm, determined, spirited refusal to be labeled "victim."

79, 80. Fundamental to this course is the concept that though you have options of physical defense available, if you are grabbed ...

77

78

79

80

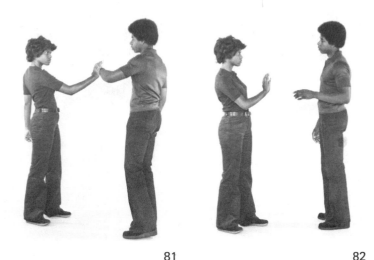

81   82

81. ...and you can divert a hostile action in a positive
manner ...

82. ...it is your inner determination, conviction and self-
reliance which are most important for assault prevention.
This photo shows how the message is conveyed in stance,
in gesture and in facial expression. This is a woman using
eye-to-eye contact, assertively making a statement of her
refusal to be bullied.

SHOUTING

Shouting is a splendid aid to self-defense. Despite the publicity
about cases in which help was not given, shouting can bring
and has brought help to intended victims of assault. Even when
shouting might not bring help, it is useful as an adjunct to
spirited resistance.

Shouting and yelling make you feel and give you the convinc-
ing appearance of a resister - a non-victim Unless a weapon is
involved, shouting, of itself, may be enough of a deterrent.
Shouting is an unexpected, and therefore disconcerting, response
to the threat of assault; most victims are silently docile.

Shout *at* the assailant. Practice using command words
and phrases as part of the self-defense training. "Stop,"
"Get away from me," "Leave me alone," and similar
shouted commands are effective, unexpected and
practical.

DEFENSE EXAMPLES

Most of the defense examples are combinations of the basic actions and many of the defenses resemble one another. This is a great advantage for practical self-defense.

With a few exceptions, which will be noted in the text, the defenses shown for practice are examples of variations in the uses of the basic defense actions. In many of the instances, the order of the actions could be changed; different hand blows might be used, other than those selected; or, a single defense action might be used repeatedly as a complete defense.

Avoid thinking of the defense examples as a rigid series of movements which must be done exactly as shown. You need only memorize a few defenses; for most situations you need not think in terms of specific defense for the specific assault. In the preceding examples of how you might respond with one wrist gripped, the order of the hand blows could be varied in a great number of ways and the kicking actions could have been given as first responses, rather than as ending actions.

WRIST GRIP DEFENSES

Like many other hostile or aggressive physical actions, wrist grips are sometimes merely annoying or they may be used in conjunction with verbal abuse, or they may be tests of docility, or part of a serious assaultive attempt.

83. In an annoying but not very serious situation, the finger-bending release might be adequate, by itself. Here, the defense action is against the thumb.

If the grab were part of a testing-for-victim-behavior action, an immediate response and determined expression would convey clearly the message: This is not a docile victim!

84   85

84, 85. Exactly the same release can be used for a wrist grab
such as shown.

The partner who is acting the role of assailant: Take a firm
grip and try to maintain it, but do not hold on when the
release action hurts! Release your grip when the defense is
applied correctly.

Defending partner: Do not use a jerky action against your
practice partner, as you would in actual defense. If you
grip the thumb with your entire hand - not merely with
your fingertips - you can break a firm grip by bending back
slowly and firmly.

86. In a more threatening or dangerous situation, you could
begin your defense with a vigorous kick into the shin, to
distract and hurt the aggressor.

87. Then, you could use the finger-bending release, or you
could make a fist of your captured hand...

88. ...and snap it free downward from between the thumb
and forefinger.

The action of the defense should be practiced in fairly slow
motion at first. Speed is not as important as vigorous,
spirited actions. Simulate the kick without making contact
on your partner.

86

87

88

One of the many variations which could be used for this defense: You might have started with a chop onto the gripping forearm, a stamp onto the instep and a second hand blow onto the nose, and then followed those actions with the wrist release action.

Practice the defense as it is shown in the photos, then practice the suggested variation. Think about additional variations possible in this situation.

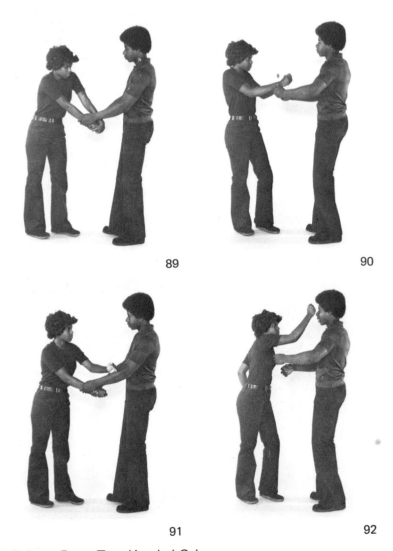

89

90

91

92

Release From Two-Handed Grip

89,90. One wrist is gripped with two hands. Make a fist of the captured hand; reach over and between the gripping arms and with a snappy, lively action, pull up and toward yourself to free the captured wrist.

91. You could precede the release action with forceful kicks into the shin and a slash onto the forearm.

92. If appropriate, you could follow the release action with a fist blow down onto the nose.

93

94

95

96

Double Wrist Grip Release

93. Both wrists are gripped. Simulate a kick into the shin to hurt and distract the assailant.

94. Push outward with your arms and hands; the reaction to your outward push will be an inward push.

95,96. Taking advantage of the inward pushing movement, bring your hands slightly inward and then up with a snappy action to effect release from between the thumbs and forefingers.

Practice the release action in slow motion. Partner who
is acting the role of assailant: Take a moderately firm grip.
Do not permit release if your partner attempts to pull back
against the strong line of your grip. Release only when the
correct action is performed and the wrists are snapped free
from between your thumbs and forefingers.

Defending partner: If you attempt to struggle free, using
force against force, you cannot escape. It is the direction
of the snappy action which effects release.

In practice, you do not have the element of surprise in your
favor. Your partner will cooperate by responding as though
you had actually kicked, once or twice, before breaking
the wrist grip. If the situation were serious, you would
precede the release action by kicking as forcefully as possible. If you were only being teased, you might try the arm
action to effect release, but if the aggressor persisted, you
might have to use a moderately forceful kick into the shin
for successful release.

Double-Wrist Grip - Rear

97. Both wrists are gripped. Using the support of the grip,
lean forward...

98. ...allowing you to deliver a forceful kick back into the
knee or shin. The kick will cause pain and distraction...

99, 100. ...allowing you to snap your arms free with a jerky
action.

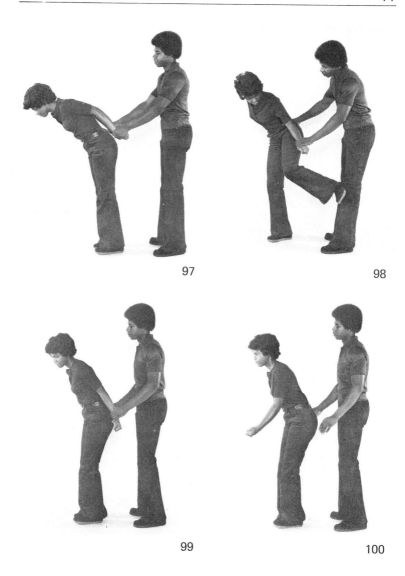

97

98

99

100

101

102

103

Second Release Example

101-103. Both wrists are gripped from the back. Start with a snappy kick into the shin, scrape down the shin and stamp onto the instep as you release one hand with a sharp downward action.

Without hesitation, step away and turn to face the assailant, ready to use hand and foot blows to effect release of the other wrist.

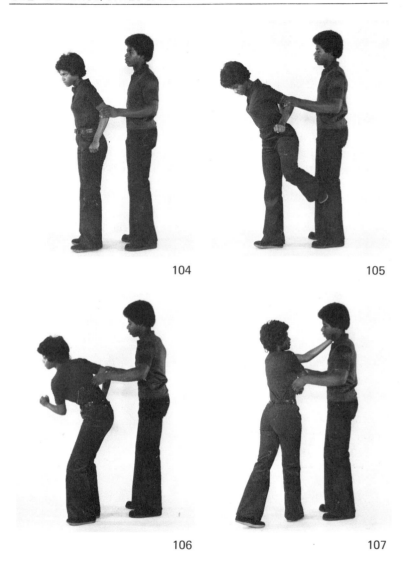

104

105

106

107

Rear Double Elbow Grip Release

104,105. Both arms are gripped at the elbows. Start with a kick into the shin, and without hesitation...

106,107. ...snap one arm forward to effect release as you turn to face the aggressor and hit and kick as necessary to free the other arm.

AVOIDANCE PROCEDURES

The following are practice procedures to help you develop
orderly responses to attempted assault and to the testing
actions and testing commands which often precede an assault.

Forward Reach

Many assault attempts made from a facing position begin
with a reaching arm. Partner taking the role of assailant:
Cue the simulated threat by reaching toward your partner.

Partner who is defending: As the reaching arm comes
toward you, TAKE A STEP BACK as you slap/parry the
reaching arm. Practice the same action, using a slash/parry.

Practice hitting outward, cross-body and downward to
deflect the reaching arm. Do not permit your partner's
hand to touch you. Alternate using your right hand and
your left hand for the parry.

108. To practice fully-released slash and parry actions
against the reaching arm, you can use a padded stick. Hit
with a spirited action, and hit as hard as you are able.
Practice the various ways of parrying and remember to
step back as you avoid the reaching "arm". Partner who
is taking the role of assailant: With the padded stick,
simulate high (face and shoulder height), middle (waist
height) and low (wrist-gripping height) reaching gestures.

As you practice the step-back-and-parry, make a verbal command or shout at the aggressor.

Partners: Check each other. The stepping back is important; it is an action which demonstrates positive refusal to accept the role of passive victim.

When both partners have practiced diverting the reaching stick "arm," increase the speed of the aggressive action somewhat; mix right and left reaches; reach for the high, middle and low body areas. With moderate practice you should be able to avoid a completed shoulder-grab, body grab, wrist grab or similar assaultive action by stepping out of range and diverting the reaching arm.

Step-and-Parry as Defense

The step-back-and-parry action can also be thought of as a defense, appropriate for use against slapping, punching, grabbing or gripping assaults. In the less serious aggressions, stepping and deflecting would be a complete defense. In the more serious kinds of assault, the deflection could be followed with appropriate kicking and/or hitting as required to complete the defense.

Response to Back Threat

As important as being able to cope with a completed assault is the ability to respond to an attempted assault *before* it is completed.

The following procedure is practiced to respond to a cue of "danger" from behind you. It is also an example of a defense.

The environment and setting in which you would respond this way would be those in which you would have reason to be wary. Among friends and family you would not respond to a touch on the shoulder by turning to block and hit.

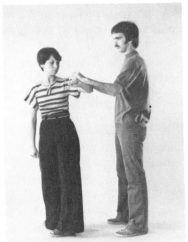

109 110

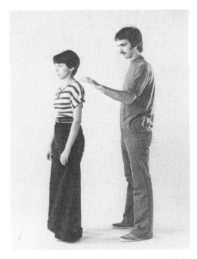

111 112

109,110. Practice this as a light shoulder grab from behind to which the defending partner responds by turning and blocking, moving only the head and upper body.

111,112. Next, practice the turn and block with more distance between the partners. After a few rehearsals your response should be quick and lively and you can step as you turn to block.

113

114

115

116

113. Your further response might be a verbal command, or you would be in position to hit and kick, if necessary.

Practice variations of the turn-block-hit actions.

114-116. As your partner cues you by touching your shoulder lightly, turn and block and hit down onto the nose.

Other variations might be: Turn and block; follow with several hand blows of your choice. Turn and block; follow with alternating hand and foot blows - two of each. Make up your own variations.

When you have rehearsed the foregoing evasion/avoidance procedures, you will be able to think in terms of actions to prevent numerous types of assaults from being completed, even if they are attempted. The turn-and-block response could avoid a back choke, a mugging attempt, a rear wrist grip, a body grip, and other, similar annoyances or serious assaults.

 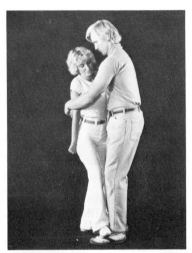

117   118

BODY GRAB DEFENSES

The best defense against a front body grab is avoidance! If you sense that a hostile action is threatened, stay out of arm's reach. Or parry the reaching arm or arms.

Rehearse the escapes from body grabs using mild release techniques and vigorous defense actions so that you could cope with annoying or serious situations.

Front Grabs

117. If you are grabbed under the arms, you can hit with your hands and feet: Against an annoying aggressor, a pushing action up under the chin, or a stepping, grinding action onto the instep with your heel would be sufficient and appropriate.

If the assailant were threatening more serious harm, you could use a thrusting vigorous hit up under the chin, any of the hand blows you have learned, combined with vigorous kicks, as needed for release.

118. If grabbed over the arms, you would be limited to the use of moderately forceful kicks against an annoying aggressor. Forceful kicking, scraping and stamping, repeated as necessary to effect release, would be the principal defense against a more threatening individual.

In the grab, as shown, you could use a knee kick into the groin. Our experience indicates that most women prefer to use the kick into the shin and onto the instep; it is an effective technique without the overtones of sexual counter-assault implicit in the groin kick.

Back Grabs

In this example of a body grab from the back, the defense might be one of the three actions, a combination of any two of them, or all three actions, repeated as necessary to effect release.

119. Against a mildly hostile or annoying person, the finger grip release could be used alone.

120. In a more serious situation, start with a forceful snap kick back into the shin...

119   120

121. ...and without hesitation, hit back into the head
or neck with your elbow, and, if necessary, use the finger-
bending release.

122   123

Over-Arm Body Grab

122. A swift, snappy kick into the shin may effect release.
Or, you can continue the defense by scraping down onto
the shin and as you get ready to stamp onto the instep,
clasp your hands together, take a deep breath...

123. ...and as you exhale suddenly, hit into the midsection with an elbow blow.

124   125

Arm Pulled Up The Back

As is true of many of the assault examples in this book, the illustrated situation could be anything from a horsing-around, half-playful non-threatening situation to a mean and harm-intended assault. The degree of force used and the ending actions of the defense should be appropriate to the particular situation.

124. Your arm is captured and pulled up your back. Reach back and place your free hand onto your captured hand and press down. This will relieve some of the pain and allow you to continue the defense.

125. Maintaining the hand pressure, kick sharply into the shin...

126   127

126. ...and without hesitation, thrust both arms straight down...

127. ...and turn to continue with hand and foot blows, if necessary, to effect a complete release and escape.

128   129

Hair Pulling

The two most common hair-pulling assaults are: Grabbing hair at the top of the head or pulling longer hair at the ends. The defense actions are similar and the photos show a combination of the pain-relieving defense.

128. If your hair is pulled at the top of your head, clamp both your hands down onto the grabbing hand and press down. If your hair is pulled at the ends, grab your own hair or the wrist of the aggressor and pull toward your head to relieve the pain.

129. Maintain your hand pressure to relieve the pain and turn and kick. If you duck down slightly before you turn, you will twist the wrist of the aggressor, aiding your defense.

130

Defense Against Kicking Assault

Stepping or jumping out of range of a kicking assault is a
good, evasive tactic. Take turns with your partner, simulating an avoidance response to a threatened kick. If you are
agile and fit, you can leap out of range of the kicking leg.
Or, practice taking a deep step to the side, or backward, as
the kick is simulated.

130. Then, practice a counter-kick defense against the kick,
with your partner using a padded stick to simulate the kicking leg. As the "leg" comes toward you, kick with the side
of your shoe, at shin height. Use a snappy, forceful kick to
deflect the assault.

Practice counter-kicking against right and left foot kicks;
alternate counter-kicks with your right foot and your left
foot.

The foregoing is also good practice to develop the ability
to deliver full-power kicks without losing your balance and
without hurting your partner.

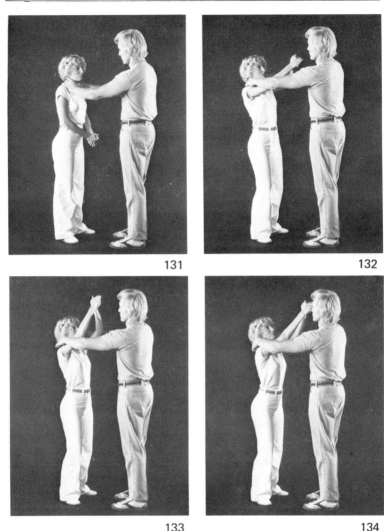

131   132

133   134

Front Choke/ Shoulder Grab Defense

131-134. Clasp your hands together (do not intertwine
your fingers) and with a forceful, quick action, thrust your
arms up between the assailant's arms with follow-through
to break the choke. Without hesitation, hit down onto the
nose with your clasped hands. If necessary, hit and kick
to complete the defense.

Against a choke, you must begin the defense with the
action which breaks the choke. If this were shoulder-
grabbing, you could choose, instead, to begin the defense
with a kick into the shin or a stamp onto the instep.

135   136

SEATED DEFENSES

Seated next to the assailant or aggressor, you have many of
the same options as you do for standing defense. Using the
appropriate responses, you can manage situations which do not
involve threat of physical harm, but are unwelcome or annoying; you can cope with insistent aggressors; and you can use
the more serious defense actions, when necessary.

135. The assertive "no" can be used in many situations
which might otherwise escalate into a more difficult or more
distressing predicament. If, in your judgment, the person
making the advance is not going to hurt you, your gesture
of refusal can be positive, definite, and unambiguous, without being grim or hostile. If your voice and your gesture
and tone of self-reliance are convincingly consistent, your
refusal will be accepted as sincere.

136. But, if necessary, you can use the finger-bending release,
gently, if that is appropriate to the situation...

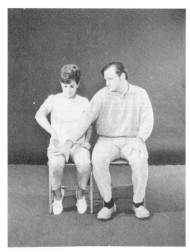
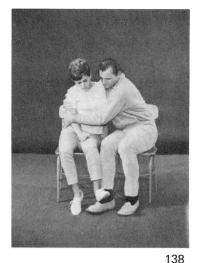

137   138

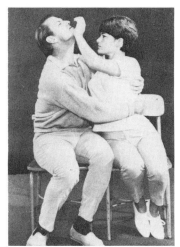

139

137. ...or, with more force, if necessary.

138. If you are grabbed, you can use the stamping kick down onto the instep, or you might need only a moderately forceful grinding action with your heel onto the instep.

139. The heel-of-palm blow can be used with as much force as is appropriate.

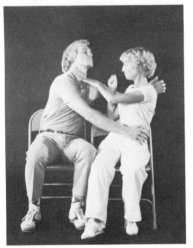 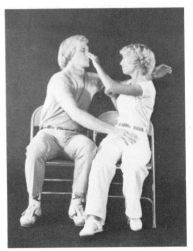

140   141

140. And for the more serious assault threats, stabbing blows into the windpipe...

141. ...or eyes can be used from a seated position.

Any of the above can be used in combination, or singly, depending on the situation encountered.

BACK ATTACKS

As you practice the procedures for responding to the threat of back chokes and grips before they are completed, you will become less vulnerable to such assaults. You practice the defenses because anxiety is diminished as competence is developed. Your attitude of self-reliance is reflected in your general appearance and behavior, making it even *less* likely that you would be chosen as a potential victim.

The combination of knowing how to avoid back attack and proficiency in coping with a completed assault is your best protection against panic .

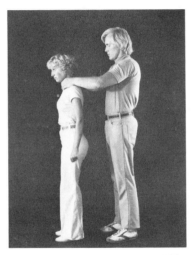

142   143

Back Choke

142. The assailant chokes in the manner shown.

143. Start the defense by relieving the choking pressure. This is one of the few instances in which the first action *must* be the one shown; if you were to turn to kick, for instance, the choking pressure might be increased by your action. First, stop the choking pressure! Grip his little fingers with both your hands...(You could break the choke by gripping and pulling one finger, but practice the more efficient defense action as shown here.)...

144   145

144. ...with a snappy action, break the choke by pulling
sharply against his little fingers...and when the choke is
broken, let go of one finger as you maintain a firm hold on
the other finger and turn...

145. ...and kick with force, into the knee or shin.

The complete defense shown here is, in all likelihood, a
longer series of actions than you would need in a real
situation. If, after breaking the choke by pulling back
on his fingers, you are free to run and have a safe place
to run, run away! There is an even stronger possibility
that your demonstration of competence would result in
the assailant running away. The complete series of actions
is taught in order to reinforce your feeling of competence.

Forearm Choke

This is a widely feared assault, often seen on television and
portrayed as a situation which renders the victim completely
helpless. Or the television version of "self-defense" for
this assault is shown: The woman pulls the assailant over
her shoulder and throws him to the ground. It would be
extremely difficult and unlikely that a throw over the
shoulder could be used in such a situation - except by a very
highly trained individual. For practical self-defense, throw-
ing over the shoulder is worse than useless, for the action
of attempting the throw increases the pressure of the choke!

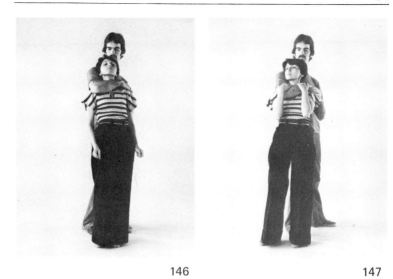

146   147

146. The assailant chokes, using the forearm, and pulls back slightly to take the defending partner off balance.

147. The first action *must* relieve the pain and danger of the choke. If the choking pressure is not reduced immediately, there is a possibility of serious injury or unconsciousness. To reduce the pressure, grip the arm with both hands and turn your head into the bend of the elbow; pull *down* with your hands and arms throughout the completion of the defense. This action relieves some of the pain and it removes the pressure from the highly vulnerable windpipe to the side of the neck.

Although it is possible to be choked unconscious with heavy pressure against the side of the neck (at the carotid artery), the risk of serious, permanent injury or fatality is reduced if the choking pressure is at the carotid artery rather than at the windpipe.

If you have a strong and cooperative partner, you can demonstrate the effectiveness of this first action. If your partner grips in the manner shown, and you grip the choking arm firmly, you could be lifted off the ground; if you maintain your hand grips with all your body weight assisting the action, you can effectively reduce the pain and pressure.

148   149

148, 149. Maintaining your hand grips firmly, kick back
into the shin and scrape down the shin with the edge of your
shoe and stamp onto the instep. Repeat the kick and scrape
and stamp several times. The space relationship between
the partners will determine which leg should be used for
kicking and which leg of the assailant is most easily used
as a target for the kicks.

The general rule is: Do what is most simple and practical.
Kicking with the edge of the shoe is most efficient; you do
not have to be able to see the leg target if you turn the side
of your shoe toward the leg and kick back with force.

Be very careful in this phase of the rehearsal with the
partner; a sharp kick into the shin is extremely painful.

150, 151. Your partner will respond to the simulated kicks
by reducing the choking grip somewhat. Maintaining the
downward pull with your hands, take a step back and pull
your head free, continuing to kick, if necessary to effect
full release.

150

151

152

153

152. When your head is free you may pull his arm sharply up his back...

153. ...and kick behind his knee as you shove with your arms.

Continue with additional kicks, if necessary to complete the defense to allow you to escape.

154   155

Hand Over Mouth

154. This is only one version of an assault made from behind in which the assailant attempts to prevent screaming or calling for help. Variations might include: Gripping around the waist or gripping the shoulder while placing a hand over the mouth or face.

155. Grip a finger, the little finger if it is available, and pull the finger with a snappy, lively action...

156. ...with enough follow-through to move the arm away...

157. ...and, without hesitation, turn...

158. ...to face the assailant and kick.

Continue with hand and foot blows and effect release of the captured wrist, using either of the releases you have already practiced.

156

157

158

ON THE GROUND

Kicking Defense

If you fall, or have been pushed down, do not attempt to arise within grabbing or hitting distance of your assailant. Your best defense is to keep your head away from reaching arms or kicking feet and use kicks until you can safely rise.

159. The partner who takes the role of assailant tries to move around into position to touch the defending partner's head with both hands. Defending partner: Swivel on your buttocks and use your hands to help you move around so that your feet are always in position to kick at the assailant's leg. As a practice procedure, you will not, of course, make contact as you kick.

160. Place your foot at your partner's knee and keep it there as you swivel around, following the attempts to move around to your head. In actual defense, a forceful kick could buckle the assailant down.

The next phase of practice is one which requires special safety concern on the part of each partner. The partner simulating the defense will kick with force and vigor; the partner simulating the assault will make a real effort to move fast enough to get around to the partner's head, but will take care to stay out of range of the kicks.

Lying Down

Practice the hand blows and front choke defense from a supine position.

161. Your partner will kneel next to you and simulate attempted choking. Break the choke with the clasped-hand thrust up between the arms, and hit onto the nose...

162. ...and follow with simulated finger stabs into the throat or eyes.

Remember that the finger stabs into throat or eyes are very high risk of injury techniques. In practice, take special care not to make contact on your partner.

159   160

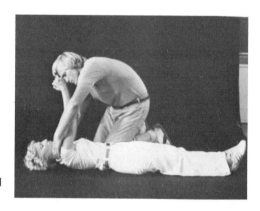

161

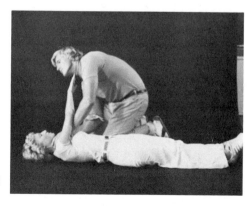

162

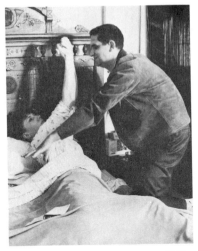

163

164

165

In Bed

163. In bed, the same types of defense actions can be used.

164. The stabbing finger blows could be used separately or
in combination with choke or grab releases.

165. Any article which is close at hand can be used to aid
your defense. Do not rely on defense aids, but if anything
is available which you can pick up and hit with, use it. Here,
she delivers a smashing blow with a metal ashtray.

166   167

Forced Entry

There are many parts of the country in which doors are not
locked during the daytime hours. The determination to
lock or not to lock doors. must be made by the individual,
and will depend upon many factors. Many of the entries
into homes are not forced - they are made easy and possible
through carelessness or lack of preparation to follow prudent,
assault-prevention procedures.

166. To set up a hypothetical situation: The door of this
home is not locked during day-time hours, but the occupant
ordinarily uses the viewer before opening the door. The
percentage of individuals who would try to force themselves
into a home after being refused admission is very small.
There is no great risk taken in this hypothetical situation.

What is exceptional is that the viewer has been used, the
caller has been refused admission, but he tries to enter
the house.

If it is possible to do it quickly, an attempt to close and
lock the door would be a prudent action.

167. Not being able to apply enough force to close the door,
the second choice defense action is to avoid being trapped
inside the house with the intruder. Using kicks, hand blows
and shouting at the intruder, push him back and away from
the door. Then, if it is possible to close and lock the door,
do so. If not, get out of the house and make as much noise
as you can, as you run to safety or the intruder runs away.

WHEN TO DEFEND AGAINST AN ARMED ASSAILANT

Gun Assault

The only prudent defense against gun assault is avoidance.
Although there are weaponless defenses against guns, they
are difficult to learn and they have limited value.

In a high percentage of gun murders, the assailant and the
victim know each other. Newspaper stories and television
dramas concentrate on the murderous stranger. In real life
it is more likely that the killer and the victim have been
involved in an intimate personal or business relationship.
Often, there has been a background of ongoing discord,
and the shooting has been preceded by less serious but
violent manifestations of disturbance and conflict.

Husbands and wives, former husbands and former wives,
parents and siblings, partners or employers, lovers or jilted
boyfriends - these are the most likely candidates for murder.

Alcohol, which is a contributing factor in many crimes of
violence, is commonly associated with gun murder. Jealousy
and revenge for some real or imagined wrong are most often
cited as motives for murder. Or the shooting occurs by
accident or in a moment of uncontrolled rage.

If you are involved with someone who owns a gun, who is
short-tempered and who harbors a grievance, you are flirting
with violent death.

You cannot expect police protection. Because of the vast
number of privately owned handguns in the United States,
the task of monitoring potentially homicidal individuals is
beyond police capability. Avoidance is the only course
which does not produce counter-violence.

Get Help!

If there is danger of gun assault, the potential victim is in
need of help. We can suggest options, but the selection of
the appropriate action must be worked out for each individual. Among the options for avoidance are: Negotiation,

counseling, legal action, separation or relocation. All of the foregoing require skilled guidance and assistance. None of the solutions for avoidance is easy, but if there is grave danger of being shot, the effort and the expense of finding a way out are worthwhile and could mean the difference between living and dying.

Armed Robbery

If either a knife or gun is used as intimidation, only, and the primary intent is robbery, it is reckless and foolish to attempt a defense. Quiet cooperation is the recommended response to armed robbery.

Knife Assault

Any defense against a knife involves a risk of injury. The major difference between a gun assault and a knife assault is that there are instances when defense against knife assault is possible. If there is a choice between passive submission to a knife assault or spirited defense, a determined attempt to defend yourself would be the safer course.

Self-Control

Those who can maintain a degree of self-control and present an appearance of composure are less likely to be harmed than those who show panic. There are those who have successfully negotiated with armed assailants by engaging in a dialogue carried on in a quiet, disciplined manner. Challenges or counter-threats of violence are self-defeating. Pleading with an armed assailant is useless.

Don't Scream

Although screaming is useful in many cases, it is not recommended when the assailant is armed. It is best not to make any noise, or sudden movements (except as noted in the knife defense which follows). Keep your hands away from pockets or purse. Do not turn your back on a gun-armed assailant; turn your back and run from a knife-armed assailant only if you are certain you can run to safety.

An armed assailant is on edge and excited. The excitement is increased when the intended victim cries, pleads or screams.

KNIFE DEFENSES

Re-read very carefully the section on armed assault and when it is more prudent to submit than to resist. The decision to defend against a knife assault threat would rest on the judgment that it is less dangerous to resist than to submit passively.

Front Threat

168. The threat is made. You decide that the defense action is the safer choice. Raise your hands. Do not make any sudden movements before your actual defense. Speak softly and maintain eye-to-eye contact. Do not look at the knife.

169. Make a subtle distracting gesture, such as is shown here - a slight movement of the hand. Or engage the assailant in a dialogue which will divert attention slightly. Take a deep breath.

170. With a sudden movement, deflect the knife-hand away and grip the wrist firmly, stiffening your arm to immobilize his hand for just the very short time necessary to...

171. ...use stabbing finger blows into the eyes.

Run away as soon as it is possible to escape. If necessary, continue with hand and foot blows, but do not attempt to disarm the assailant. Only professionals in law enforcement or institutions are required to subdue, disarm and control an armed person; the citizen need only escape with as little harm as is possible.

168

169

170

171

Back Threat

A knife attack threat made from the back is more intimidating and more difficult to cope with. If the primary objective of the encounter is robbery, and the weapon is being used to discourage resistance to the theft - do *not* resist! A defense against a knife threat is made when the only other option is being cut!

The situation simulated here is a threat to cut or harm; it is not an attempted robbery.

172. The threat is made.

173. Put up your hands immediately and, if possible, make conversation in a quiet voice. Try to give the impression of remaining calm. Do not make any sudden movements until you are ready to start the defense. If possible, turn your head slowly and slightly, to look at the assailant. But if you cannot, the defense is the same; with a sudden and vigorous action, turn and block with your forearm...

174, 175. ...and without hesitation, continue turning to face the assailant and grip his arm, pushing it away from you as you fingerstab into the eyes.

Do *not* attempt to grip the knife. Do *not* attempt to disarm the assailant.

Continue with kicking and hand blows as necessary to complete the defense and escape.

172

173

174

175

176   177

DEFENSE AIDS

We do not advise reliance on any type of defense aid. The
individual who depends on a whistle or a can of spray or any
other kind of device is likely to feel more helpless if the aid
is not at hand or fails to function.

Many of the devices advertised as alternatives to self-defense
are illegal in some states, defective in many instances, and
unless they are at hand every moment, they are of no value
whatsoever.

If an object is at hand, easily available and you can get a
firm grasp on it, you may consider using stick-like objects,
such as a broom or umbrella, or articles commonly carried in
a handbag.

Stick Aids

The two most effective actions you can use with a stick-
like object such as a broom, mop, umbrella or cane, are
jabbing and blocking.

176. The broom is held firmly with both hands. The
wooden end is thrust forward with a jabbing action.

177. The umbrella is held firmly with both hands and
used to block a reaching arm.

The uses of the broom and umbrella are interchangable. Either can also be used to deliver whipping-type blows into the side of the neck, in which case it is held with one hand. The advantage of using a two-handed grip is that there is less likelihood of losing the stick weapon.

Purse Weapons

Many of the articles in your handbag can be used as aids to defense. Or they may simply be displayed in a manner which indicates that you are aware of possible hostile action and are prepared to cope with it.

As with other defense aids, do not come to rely on them; however, you can develop the prudent habit of holding your keys in your hand as you go from your home to your car and when you leave your car to approach your doorway.

178. The tooth-edge of a comb can be used with a scraping action across the face.

179. The sharp end of a rat-tail comb or brush can be jabbed into the side of the neck.

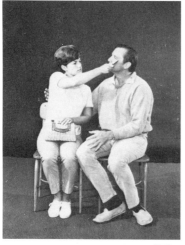 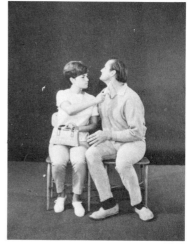

178   179

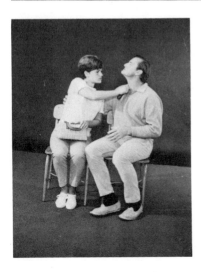

180. For the most serious danger, a key can be jabbed into the throat or eyes.

If you are in an elevator, alone with someone who makes you feel uncomfortable, reach into your handbag and grip some article which makes you appear prepared to take some action. Keep your hand inside the purse, unless you need to defend yourself - don't give away your plan of action; the element of surprise always helps !

More Than One Assailant

If more than one person threatens assault, spirited resistance is imperative. Two assailants who select a woman victim are not brave; they depend on frightened women to submit without making any effort to protect themselves.

Resistance, in such cases, may not be 100% successful, but hopeless submission is a 100% guarantee of assault.

Two Assailants Facing

Select the larger person or the one who appears to be the leader and kick with full force, using the stamping kick into the knee. Stay out of fist range. Try to move out to the side of the person you are kicking and use him as a shield between you and the other assailant. Avoid coming between them. If you can move around behind him, kick into the back of the knee with force, as shown in photo 54.

Scream, continue kicking, and move around to the side or behind them. It is highly likely that the assailants would not persist after the first vigorous kick. But, in practice, continue as though it were necessary to kick the second assailant, too. Carry on the defense until you can escape.

One Holding, One Threatening

If one person holds you and the other threatens, begin the defense by kicking at the person who is not holding. When that assailant has been hurt, kick into the shin of the assailant holding you and continue the defense to effect release (photos 119-123). Do not start the defense against the person holding until the front assailant has been stopped.

Dog for Defense?

Any dog, even a small one, may be a deterrent to assault or entry, but you must not expect or depend upon a dog to protect you unless it has been trained to do so.

A trained guard dog is not a pet or a companion. It is not a children's playmate. A guard dog is only obedient to those it has been trained to obey. Owning a guard dog means taking care that neighbors, visitors, guests and especially neighbors' children are protected from the dog. Having a guard dog is a big responsibility.

A yapping small dog is a deterrent, but it is also a nuisance. Pet dogs sometimes develop a protective attitude toward family members, but you cannot rely on it.

The decision to have a dog for protection must rest on individual circumstances, feelings and needs. If you are not a dog owner, weigh the responsibilities against the advantages before you make a decision.

Defense Against Dogs

If you cannot avoid coming close to a dog which appears to be unfriendly, prepare to take command of the situation.

Dogs respond to command, in both senses of the word. Large dogs, especially, are likely to have had training to obey certain commands made in a commanding tone. The common command words which they are trained to obey are: DOWN, STAY, and SIT. But it is not merely the words to which they respond, it is the tone and volume of the voice in which they are given. Use words which are familiar to them and avoid using phrases such as "go away" or "leave me alone" to which they are not accustomed.

Do not shriek. Try not to betray your fear. Most dogs, if commanded in the proper manner, will retreat or keep their distance.

If you have a coat or sweater, wrap it around one arm and hold that arm out in front of you.

If you are being rushed by an attacking dog: Parry the dog's head and then be prepared to kick into the throat. Or begin the defense by kicking into the throat and continue kicking until the dog runs away.

If a dog has got hold of you, do not try to pull yourself free; if you do, it will intensify the tearing action of the dog's teeth. Instead, push in the same direction as it is pulling and as you push, kick into its throat, if you can, or if necessary, use finger stabs into its eyes.

If you are bitten by a dog, you must make note of its appearance and the exact location of the incident. If you know the dog's owners, they must immediately take the dog in for testing to determine whether or not the dog is rabid. If you do not know the dog's owner, report to the police without delay and they will assist in trying to locate the dog and its owner. If you do not do this, or if you delay, you may have to undergo anti-rabies treatment. An untreated bite from a rabid dog could result in severe illness or even death. If the dog is not rabid, that treatment is not necessary.

The Missing Kick

There can hardly be any young woman who has not been told that a kick into the groin is her best defense. We do not agree.

Kicking into the groin has limited value. Kicking into the groin cannot be done unless you are very close in to the assailant and directly in front of him. If you are not close in, you should not move in within fist hitting or grabbing reach. There are many situations in which a groin kick is not possible. There are times when a groin kick would not be appropriate.

The most compelling argument against the groin kick comes from our women students: They consider a kick into the groin to be a vicious, sexual counter-assault. Overwhelmingly, they prefer to use alternative defense actions, such as a kick into the shin or knee.

Those girls and women who have been told that they need only know how to kick into the groin or poke into the eyes are left with all-or-nothing alternatives. They can use either the most serious and high-risk-of-injury tactics, or they can do nothing. This leaves them without resources for coping with the less serious aggressive acts. It leaves them without resources for responding to incipient aggression.

Kicking into the groin is least effective for the situation in which it is most commonly recommended - sexual advances made by a man who is not threatening violence, but who is persistent to the point of coercion. If a woman, especially a young woman, has no choice except unwilling submission or extreme defense actions, she may submit rather than use eye stabs or kicking into the groin.

Having realistic choices means knowing defense techniques which are appropriate for the least violent as well as the most serious kinds of coercion and assault.

Biting & Scratching

Biting or scratching an assailant is better than no resistance, but not as effective as more orderly defenses. Biting is repugnant to many. Biting or scratching must be done from close in; they are not defense actions of first choice.

GUNS FOR SELF-DEFENSE?

The practical and ethical arguments against owning handguns for self-defense far outweigh the possible advantages for the lay citizen.

A gun, or any other weapon, is not protection unless it is carried at all times, or is easily accessible and ready to fire. If it is easily accessible to you, it is easily accessible to others, including children.

The guns which are bought for self-defense are actually used to kill children, wives, lovers, husbands, parents and neighbors more frequently than they are used against an assailant. A fourteen-year study in the Cleveland, Ohio area demonstrated that householders who armed themselves to protect their homes, shot and killed 17 robbers and intruders between 1958 and 1972. During the same period in the same area, 102 family members, friends and neighbors were killed by handguns. Gun owners were responsible for killing six relatives or friends for each intruder shot and killed.

Of the annual shooting deaths which occur in our country, a majority are murders of rage or accidental killings. The slogan which implies that people are responsible for murder and that the murder would occur without the weapon is a distortion of the facts. Children who shoot their brothers in an instant of rage or by accident are unlikely to commit murder by other means.

Advocates of uncontrolled handgun ownership make it seem that the regulation of handguns is a controversial issue. Reliable polls, including a 1975 Gallup survey, revealed that 66% of the American people living in cities of more than a million population are in favor of handgun regulation.

Communities which value peace and the rule of law cannot condone the uncontrolled ownership of handguns. The alternatives are *not* the control of guns *or* the control of criminals; our communities must manage both. Police officers are in greater danger of being shot when they respond to family disputes than when they are dealing with criminals. People living in large metropolitan areas are becoming increasingly aware that they are in grave danger of violence from ordinary citizens who carry guns.

In our Constitution there is no guarantee of the individual's right to bear arms. Article II of the United States Constitution begins with the words: "A *well-regulated** militia..." Few handgun owners belong to any kind of militia.

HOME SAFETY

It is worrisome nonsense to suppose that you can make your home entry-proof - without making it into a prison - no matter what the scare-merchants try to sell you for the purpose.

The prudent procedure is to set up deterrents. Most entries are made into homes where no obstacles or deterrents of any kind have been installed: Doors and windows are left open. Children or women open the door and permit strangers to enter. Back doors are neglected. Sliding doors are not secured.

The hours and times when you should keep your doors locked will be different in different areas, neighborhoods and at different seasons. Evaluate your individual situation. Decide when it is prudent, in your case, to keep your doors locked and then *make a habit* of this safety procedure.

Keep your windows closed and locked when it is sensible and prudent and during the hours and circumstances when it is appropriate.

Large sliding glass doors are common in the West. They should be secured at the times and hours when other doors and windows are locked. Your sliding door should be fitted with a bolt or pin lock which prevents lifting it out of its track.

If you are not certain that your locks are secure, your neighborhood hardware merchant can advise you.

*italics, ours

When your doors are locked, you should have an easy way of
seeing and talking to anyone who knocks. A simple, inexpensive viewer can be installed in most doors. You should have a
sturdy safety chain on each door which leads outside. You
should get into the habit of looking through the viewer
before you open the door.

Courtesy vs. Safety

It is too bad that we cannot freely open doors to anyone who
knocks. Acknowledging the reality does not mean that you
have to barricade yourself. The violent stranger does not *break*
in as often as he is *allowed*, even *invited*, to enter the apartment
or house.

You can be alert and aware without being suspicious of everybody. During the day there are legitimate callers whose services
or merchandise you might wish to use or buy.

But even during the day you should be cautious. Service calls
are almost always arranged for in advance. Be wary of someone who claims to be serviceman if you were not expecting
the call. Ask to see identification, or telephone your building
superintendent or the company to confirm the call and the
credentials of the caller. If you cannot confirm, do not allow
the person in your home. You do not have to make excuses
or give a reason. It is your home and you are the one who
decides who may and who may not enter it. Women who
have been reared to be courteous to polite strangers should
be reminded that the men who might be dangerous present
themselves in a manner which does not arouse suspicion. They
make plausible stories about offering or needing help. You
can be a kindly and helpful person without allowing a
stranger in your home. Make a phone call, or step outside to
give directions, or refer the person to a home or apartment
where you are sure that more than one member of the
family is in.

If you have allowed someone into your home and you become
uncomfortable in his presence, ask him to leave. If he does
not leave, take immediate action: Telephone, get out of the
house, or be prepared to defend yourself. If you are firm and
positive, there is little likelihood that he would refuse to leave.
If you are embarrassed and apologetic, he will take that as a
sign of vulnerability.

Anyone with a legitimate reason for coming into your home will not resent your caution. It is more prudent to refuse entry to a legitimate caller than it is to invite possible danger into your home.

If a person at the door is, or purports to be, a messenger or delivery man whom you do not expect or recognize, take the message without removing the safety chain. If a package is too large to fit through the opening, ask that the package be left at the door and you can get it after he leaves. This is a particularly prudent procedure at night if you are alone.

There are salesmen who make calls at night because they expect more people to be home or because they want to talk to husband and wife. Unless you have arranged for an evening appointment with the representative of a reputable company, do not let a salesman in at night if you are alone! If he persists, that is reason alone to refuse him. If a salesman is persistent, report it to his company.

The Un-secret Key

Everybody knows the "secret" hiding places for keys. The first places an intruder will look are: Under the door mat, over the door jamb and in the nearest plant pot. If you must leave a key outside your apartment or home, use some imagination to hide it and do not tell anyone except the person for whom the key is intended.

Lights Deter

Inside and outside lights are a deterrent. Prowlers prefer the dark. Leave lights on at night, even when you are away from home. Change the location of the lights from time to time. Outside lights should be placed where they illuminate entrances and walkways from garage to front door. Automatic switches are not expensive; they can be used to turn lights on and off when you are away. Install switches for turning on outside lights from inside the house as well as outside. You can illuminate the area you are going to walk to before you leave the house.

Elevator

If you find yourself in the lobby with a stranger, let him take the elevator and wait for it to return for you. If you are in an elevator and someone gets on whose presence makes you uncomfortable, get off at the next floor. If you stay on the elevator, face the individual, stand near the call buttons ready to press the "alarm." Look alert and aware. You may put your hand in your purse, ready to use keys or comb as a striking weapon, if you wish. But your best protection is a self-controlled, alert appearance.

Plan Ahead To Get Help

Unless you think about it and prepare for it you may not be able to get help, even when it is readily available. In a panic, you might forget how easy it is to get help by phone.

Some communities have an all-purpose phone number which can be used for any emergency. That number should be attached to your telephone. If you do not have an all-emergency phone number, attach the phone numbers for police and fire departments to your phone. When you do not have emergency numbers, dial the operator; telephone operators are trained to get help if you give them the relevant information. The formula for getting help is: "I am calling from (phone number); I am at (address)"; then, a brief description of the emergency.

Safety for Singles

All the foregoing advice applies to single girls and women; just more so! It is particularly important to you to develop the habit of safety and prudent behavior so you do not have to brood about your vulnerability.

Do not broadcast or make general knowledge of the fact that you live alone. Be particularly careful to keep shades drawn at night. Your listing in the telephone book should be by initial and last name. When you talk to strangers on the telephone don't volunteer the information that you live alone or that you are alone at that moment. Telling a stranger that you are alone can be interpreted as an invitation.

Safety On The Street

If you can possibly avoid it, do not walk alone at night on a dark street. This may sound like kindergarten advice, yet many women ignore this basic rule of safety on the street. There is safety in company. Rarely are two women attacked; it is the lone person who is selected as a victim. If you work hours which make it necessary for you to be out at night, the buddy system might be your solution. It is worth the time and energy to take a route of comparative safety rather than take the shortest way home. A street which is lighted and on which there are people is much safer to walk on than a dark and lonely street.

If you cannot avoid walking alone on dark streets, take precautions which will minimize the danger of assault. Keep away from the building side of the street, walk well toward the curb; this minimizes the possibility of being grabbed from a doorway or building entrance. Carry a whistle, but do not *depend* on it.

If you think you are being followed, you *must* turn to look, otherwise you are vulnerable to back attack. If you feel threatened by what you see when you turn around, decide what is the most prudent behavior. Is there a safe place to go? If you can get to a lighted street with people, a store, a gas station, anyplace which offers protection, walk briskly toward it. Brisk walking denotes composure and does not betray fear; running is a good idea if you can outrun the man. Don't behave like an easy victim. No matter what the situation is, you are safer if you face it and evaluate it.

Driving Safety

The basic safety rule for drivers is SAFETY CHECK YOUR CAR. Auto trouble can strand you in strange places, far from help. Always carry change for a phone call.

When you are driving alone at night or in remote areas, or whenever there is a possibility of danger, follow the procedures which will minimize the possibility of attack. Keep the windows rolled up and the safety buttons down. If you keep the driver's side window open, be ready to roll it up.

If you are driving alone and someone signals that there is something wrong with your car, do *not* stop or let him in. Drive immediately to the nearest gas station or to some area where there are people before you check it out. Better to risk damage to your car than risk damage to yourself.

Remember your horn, it can bring help if you need it. In mental rehearsal, start the engine if the horn won't work with the engine off.

If you are driving alone and see someone who is apparently having car trouble, DO NOT STOP. You can be helpful to a stranded driver without risk to yourself. Note the location of the car and its make and color. Drive to the nearest gas station or telephone and report the trouble.

It is inexpensive insurance to park in a parking lot rather than on a dark street. Getting into a car on a dark street is an occasion for being particularly alert. Carry your keys ready so that you are not standing there fumbling for them. When you get out of your car at home, have your house keys ready. Leave a light on to illuminate the door you use.

HITCHHIKING

Hitchhiking is a high-risk activity. Sexual assault is associated with hitchhiking more than any other single circumstance. Those who choose to hitchhike in spite of the risks involved should be aware of the factors which intensify the danger and of the procedures and behavior which decrease the danger of assault.

The girl who thinks she has a "right" to hitchhike may encounter a man who thinks he has a "right" to assault anyone heedless enough to get into his car. The driver who picks up a girl with the intention of assault assumes that from the moment she accepts the ride, she is vulnerable and he is in control. He infers that she is aware of the risk and has chosen to ignore it or that she is too naive to acknowledge the possibility of danger.

The New York Mayor's Task Force on Rape has a single
sentence with respect to hitchhiking: Never hitch a ride with
anyone.

We agree that that is the best and most prudent advice! Since
many young women are still hitchhiking - and your daughter,
or you, may be one of them - we offer the following guidelines
for decreasing the risk:

Dress

If you are planning to hitchhike, dress in an appropriate manner.
Hitching in a bikini or see-through blouse will be interpreted
as provocation or invitation. You have a right to dress as you
wish, but you must consider the environment. A bikini on the
beach does not have the same connotation as it does on the
highway.

Before Getting In

Don't accept a ride with someone who has driven past, given
you the once-over and come back to pick you up. You don't
have to give a reason or excuse! Just don't get in.

Before you get in a car which has stopped for you, take a few
seconds to check out the car and driver.

If the handle of the passenger door is missing - don't get in.

Look into the back to see if there is someone there.

Don't get in if there is more than one person in the car.

If there is a smell of liquor, or there are beer cans or a liquor
bottle - don't get in.

If pornographic material is visible - don't get in.

Ask the driver where he is going. Don't get in unless he is
going in your direction. Do not accept a ride from someone
who offers to change directions or destination for you.

Be prepared to ask the driver to stop and let you out. The
ability to make this statement in a firm and positive manner
has averted hitchhiker assault.

If the driver speeds or drives erratically, tell him to stop and let you out.

Keep the conversation neutral. If the driver begins to talk about a subject with sexual overtones, or is overly inquisitive about your personal life, he may be testing. If you are not able to steer the conversation away from such subjects, tell him to stop and let you out.

Let the driver know that you have friends who expect to meet you at a specific place at a fairly definite time.

If the driver turns off the road, tell him to stop the car immediately and let you out. No shortcuts and no detours!

Assailants who have picked up hitchhikers are very likely to obey a command to stop and let them out. They, like other assailants, are looking for safe, docile, helpless victims. Do not plead; command!

DO NOT JUMP OUT OF A MOVING CAR unless there is no alternative! A car accident could be just as dangerous as an assault.

If the driver does not stop:

In traffic, plan to get out at the first traffic stop.

Plan to scream out of the window the first time there is someone to hear or see you.

Blow the horn. If he attempts to stop you, try to pull the key out of the ignition or put the gears into neutral.

Keep your hands away from the steering wheel and do not hit the driver while the car is moving.

The best chance of averting attempted assault is to be aware of the risk and respond to the first hints of possible trouble. If you respond positively and forthrightly the moment you feel uncomfortable, you could prevent serious danger.

Giving rides to hitchhikers is almost as risky as hitchhiking. Encouraging women to pick up women hitchhikers is very poor advice. If you want to reduce the possibility of assault and robbery while you are driving - don't pick up strangers!

SEXUAL ASSAULT

The feminist movement must be credited with breaking through the barriers of contempt, indifference and traditional hostility to the victims of rape. Currently, the police, the courts and the community are recognizing that sympathetic handling, medical treatment and financial and emotional support must be given to victims. But support for victims is not a substitute for programs of prevention.

The media have exploited the growing concern for rape victims by presenting sensational coverage of the most frightening and vicious instances of sexual assault. Victims are shown as completely helpless. Vengeance and punishment are the implied remedies.

The Fine Line

Rape is not a single offense; it is a continuum of offenses. Like other manipulative actions, rape ranges from situations involving little or no physical force to crimes of vicious assault.

At the lower end of the scale, where the least amount of physical force is used, there is an invisible border between seduction and rape. Like the attendant problems of unwanted pregnancy and venereal disease, the problem of seduction/rape will not yield to scolding, threats or punishment.

Solutions require forthrightness in male/female relationships, forthrightness and education about health and body functions, forthrightness about the consequences of sexual activity.

Unwelcome sexual advances can be stopped with assertive behavior and with a minimum use of the physical defenses. The techniques for dealing with seduction/rape are no different from those of dealing with any annoying, demeaning or humiliating actions in which physical harm is not the prime objective. The most serious obstacles to understanding and acting on this are the ambiguous and rape-provoking social attitudes which reduce girls and women to manipulated objects. Boys and men "score" and make "conquests"; girls

and women "give in," "surrender," "capitulate." There is a
virtual industry profiting from reinforcing the view that
woman's greatest joy is in "surrender." The language is an
accurate reflection of the social definition of an adversary
relationship between men and women. Men make the
decisions and must persuade women to comply - with as
little or as much force as is required.

The girls and women who accept these ideas, or who have
not thought about them seriously, are vulnerable to seduction/
rape. An annoying or unwelcome sexual advance can be
stopped with assertive, forthright refusal. But it must be
stopped at the *first indication* of the intention. If it is not
stopped then, it becomes more difficult and complicated to
deal with. It is reckless to engage in sexual play and expect
to avoid sexual intercourse unless limits are clearly defined
and accepted beforehand. It is reckless to pretend to accept
sexual advances if you expect to avoid sexual relations. It is
demeaning and insulting to women to suggest that they use
deceit and pretense as a way of coping with attempted rape.

There is only one honest answer to an invitation to sexual
relations: It is either "yes" or "no." Equivocating is
dishonest, provocative and confusing.

If assertive refusal is not enough, you might have to use the
same kinds of defense actions which would be used for any
other kind of unpleasant, but not dangerous, aggression.

The Terrible Stranger

When women think about rape, they are likely to think of it
as vicious assault by a terrifying stranger. In more than half
of the reported cases of sexual assault, the victim and the
assailant know each other. Rape/murder is not a common
occurrence, but one would never know that from media
accounts of rape.

Women have a fear of violent rape out of proportion to its
occurrence and they feel helpless to a degree which does not
correspond to reality.

The same defense actions which would be appropriate for any serious assault would be appropriate as protection against sexual assault. The same rules of prudent behavior to avoid assault apply to avoidance of sexual assault.

Vicious rape has more in common with child-beating than it does with seduction. Vicious rape is an act of brutal domination and so is the act of child abuse. In both cases, the chosen victim is a stand-in for powerful events or persons which the offender cannot control. So he selects a *safe* object - child or woman - on which to vent his rage and frustration. Children have no recourse. Women can refuse to be manipulated objects.

The only exception would be when confronted by an armed assailant. Submission might then be the most prudent behavior. Even so it is significant to note that women with the highest degree of self-esteem suffer the least emotional trauma if they are rape victims; women with low self-esteem suffer the most.

We come back to the opening paragraphs of this book: Prevention of seduction/rape and of sexual assault rests on foundations of self-worth and self-reliance. If you are willing to make decisions for yourself and are confident of your right to assert yourself, you will be able to avoid rape/ seduction and cope with most threats of sexual assault.

The 95% + Solution

It does not invalidate this course to acknowledge that there are some situations for which no amount of preparation can prepare you and that there are some situations in which a defense could be made only by a highly trained expert. It is not productive to fret over those exceptional cases. It is uncommon, therefore newsworthy, when complete strangers assault without provocation and without any possibility of defense or escape. Yet these are the bizarre and terrifying instances which are held up to the public as examples.

Sensational emphasis on unavoidable assaults has the effect of making us worry about the small percentage of dangers we cannot control or avert. Instead, we should be emphasizing the far greater percentage of those we *can* cope with and which we *can* prevent.

INDEX

ALICE McGRATH is a specialist in the subject area of self-defense for girls and women. Her teacher was Bruce Tegner. She has been writing, lecturing, teaching, publishing and consulting in this field since 1957.

In 1967, with Bruce Tegner, she developed a special course of self-defense appropriate for physical education classes. She introduced the new course at the California Women's Physical Education Workshop at California Polytechnic College, San Luis Obispo, an annual graduate credit program for secondary school teachers. This was the first practical self-defense course widely adopted in schools in California. In 1968, 1970 and 1972, she returned to the Workshop to present the course.

She is the co-author of two previous books on self-defense for women, both of which titles are replaced by this present work. The earlier books were based on the course presented in 1967; this book is an extension and development of the ideas and techniques of that course. Her most significant contribution to the field of women's self-defense is the linking of assertion training concepts to assault prevention. She is also the co-author of SELF-DEFENSE for YOUR CHILD, a book for the use of parents, teachers and counselors of elementary school age boys and girls.

With Bruce Tegner, Alice McGrath has conducted extensive in-service training programs for teachers throughout California and in Wisconsin, Nevada and Oregon, with the objective of preparing physical education teachers to instruct self-defense. She holds a California Community Colleges teaching credential, and in addition to her principal activity as a publisher/writer, she teaches at Ventura College and Oxnard College, in California. In the subject field of the martial arts, Alice McGrath is a contributor and consultant to the *Encyclopedia Americana.*

BRUCE TEGNER is a specialist in sport and self-defense forms of weaponless fighting skills. He is regarded as this country's outstanding authority, teacher and innovator in the field.

He was born in Chicago, Illinois, in 1929. Both his parents were professional teachers of judo and jujitsu and they began to instruct him when he was two years old! Until he was eight, his mother and father trained him in fundamentals; after that he was taught by Asian and European experts. At the age of ten, he began to teach - assisting in the instruction of children's classes at his parents' school. At seventeen, he was the youngest second-degree (nidan) black belt on record in the United States.

In a field where most individuals study only one specialty, Bruce Tegner's background is unusual. His education covered many aspects of weaponless fighting as well as stick and sword techniques. At the age of twenty-one, after he had become California state judo champion, he gave up competition to devote himself completely to teaching, research, writing and teacher-training.

In the U.S. armed forces, Mr. Tegner trained instructors to teach weaponless combat, he taught military police tactics and he coached sport judo teams. He has trained actors and devised fight scenes for films and TV. From 1952 to 1967 he operated his own school in Hollywood where he taught men, women, children, exceptionally gifted students and blind and disabled persons.

He has devised many special courses, among them, basic self-defense units which are taught in physical education classes.

Bruce Tegner has many books in print in this subject field. He has been highly praised by professionals in physical education and library journals and by psychologists. The books range from basic, practical self-defense to exotic forms of fighting for experts and enthusiasts. They are used as texts for physical education classes, in recreation centers, by law enforcement training academies and by individuals throughout the world. Editions of Tegner titles have been published in French, German, Spanish, Portuguese and Dutch.

Currently, Bruce Tegner teaches classes at Moorpark College and Ventura College in California. He is a contributor to the *Encyclopedia Americana*.

BRUCE TEGNER books are on sale at bookstores and magazine stands throughout the world. If your local dealer does not stock the titles you want, you may order directly from the publisher. For free descriptive brochure, write to:

THOR PUB. CO.
BOX 1782
VENTURA, CALIF. 93001